T0366752

"In the tradition of Alexis de Tocqueville and William Least Heat-Moon, Emily Wallace invites readers for a ride-along that reveals truths about people and the roads they take. Her strengths are different: She can draw and paint! She's funny! She's been to Weeki Wachee! But the results are just as insightful. *Road Sides* is flush with intellectual curiosity and small-town wonder and begs a full tank and an open road."

—**JOHN T. EDGE,** author of *The Potlikker Papers:*
*A Food History of the Modern South*

"This personal tour of the South is both fascinating and beautiful to look at. I'm craving a road trip to check out all the exciting sites and snacks."

—**JULIA ROTHMAN,** author of *Hello NY:*
*An Illustrated Love Letter to the Five Boroughs*

"America's highways have always reflected our culture, and Wallace's beautifully illustrated book shows us there are still regional foods and off-the-beaten-path restaurants that deserve our attention and our patronage."

—**EDWARD LEE,** chef and author of *Buttermilk Graffiti: A Chef's*
*Journey to Discover America's New Melting-Pot Cuisine*

"Only the brilliant Emily Wallace could capture the complex, curious, delightful, disturbing, and delicious roadside landscapes of the modern South, where pop culture, inventive food entrepreneurs, and hungry travelers have intersected for decades. Wallace's unmistakable artistry, humor, and smarts enliven our take on these beloved venues and their hold on the southern imagination and palate."

—**MARCIE COHEN FERRIS,** author of *The Edible South:*
*The Power of Food and the Making of an American Region*

"*Road Sides* is an easygoing but illuminating guide to the region's earnest quirkiness and made this lapsed southerner nostalgic, in the best possible way."

—**JANE MOUNT,** author of *Bibliophile: An Illustrated Miscellany*

# ROAD SIDES

# ROAD SIDES

An **ILLUSTRATED COMPANION**
to **DINING** and **DRIVING**
in the **AMERICAN SOUTH**

## EMILY WALLACE

UNIVERSITY OF TEXAS PRESS ⬮ AUSTIN

**The publication of this book was made possible by a generous contribution from the University of Texas Press Advisory Board.**

Illustrations and creative direction: Emily Wallace
Design and typesetting: Amanda Weiss

Requests for permission to reproduce material
from this work should be sent to:
Permissions
University of Texas Press
P.O. Box 7819
Austin, TX 78713-7819
utpress.utexas.edu/rp-form

♾ The paper used in this book meets the minimum requirements
of ANSI/NISO Z39.48-1992 (R1997) (Permanence of Paper).

Names: Wallace, Emily, author.
Title: Road sides : an illustrated companion to dining and
    driving in the American South / Emily Wallace.
Description: First edition. | Austin : University of Texas Press, 2019. |
    Includes bibliographical references and index.
Identifiers: LCCN 2019007785
    ISBN 978-1-4773-1656-6 (cloth : alk. paper)
    ISBN 978-1-4773-1933-8 (library e-book)
    ISBN 978-1-4773-1934-5 (nonlibrary e-book)
Subjects: LCSH: Southern States—Guidebooks. | Southern
    States—Description and travel. | Automobile travel—Southern
    States—Guidebooks. | Southern States—History, Local. |
    Curiosities and wonders—Southern States.
Classification: LCC F207.3 .W28 2019 | DDC 917.504—dc23
LC record available at https://lccn.loc.gov/2019007785

doi:10.7560/316566

FOR MW, LA, AND RW —
THE LETTERS THAT MEAN THE MOST.

# INTRODUCTION

By Arkansas we were over it. The four of us girls—all cousins coping with middle school—had already stretched ourselves into a "T" for Tennessee while standing on the lawn at Graceland. My curly hair scribbled its way out of a terrycloth scrunchie, frazzled by hours in a cramped van. Still, our uncle, whose idea it had been, snapped a picture as other tourists looked on. And in Arkansas, the second state we visited on a road trip with extended family, he vowed to do the same. That's how my cousins and I found ourselves in a parking lot debating who'd be held horizontally to create the crossbar for the letter "A." (My youngest cousin, Katie, lost the argument.)

But by Texas we'd given in and T'd up without complaint. Maybe we'd been worn down, having clocked more than a thousand miles since leaving our homes in North Carolina. Maybe we were feeling especially obedient (my cousin had just knocked a bust off the wall at the National Cowboy Hall of Fame in Oklahoma City, which prompted a long talk between the adults in our group and a pack of security guards wearing cowboy hats). Or maybe—most likely—we were simply enjoying ourselves far from the founts of our early teenage angst. Viewed through the tinted windows of my aunt's teal Oldsmobile van, the road stretched out before us—sometimes, admittedly, in dull sweeps, but also often in awe-inspiring

WORLD'S OLDEST HAM

CURED *in* 1902
*by* P.D. Gwaltney Jr. & Co.,Inc.
SMITHFIELD, VA.

*& WILL TRAVEL FOR HAM*

spans. We'd happen upon a striking vista or a splendid ice cream stand (which, at the time, they all seemed to be) and find ourselves giddy with discovery once again. In Texas we tried *beef* barbecue. In Arizona I bought *cactus* candy!

Meals marked time and kept us going, giving us something to anticipate. "We'll get lunch outside of Dallas," my aunt promised. Or, "We'll find dinner in two hundred miles." Between stops, we snacked on packets of Nab sandwich crackers we'd packed for the trip and swigged southern sodas we bought at gas stations nowhere near home. I *swear* that a message printed under the lid of a Pepsi bottle made me a finalist to win a car, but there's no proof, and no car. Someone threw the drink away while cleaning out the van.

Food also provided entry into different communities without veering too far off the highway. For a bunch of North Carolinians, that beef barbecue signaled just how long we'd traveled. Even the brands of chips we bought and the toppings on hot dogs we ate were signifiers of different places and people. Roadside fare (what might be defined as accessible, convenient, or portable food) acquaints us with stories knit together—or cut off by—a network of highways. For my cousins and me, this first major road trip provided a mighty introduction and an open invitation for further conversation.

And so it was that by the time we circled back to North Carolina after two weeks of travel, we had pretty much become willing participants, bending ourselves into letters near each border. We were smitten with the road and the wider world it led us to see and experience. Our dumb formations commemorated the places we'd been, as did the postcards I'd sent home, the photos I'd taken, and all the tchotchkes I'd picked up along the route.

I've driven thousands of miles since then in many cars, some better than others. My first, a clunky Buick dubbed Silver Death, proved a rather adventurous mate. The trips have been long (to Florida) and short (to the town two over). They've been embarked upon for fun (to hang with a mermaid) and research (to visit a giant strawberry-shaped building). They've been direct (a straight shot across I-40) and detoured (will travel for ham). At times they've even been derailed (read: lost). But there are miles left to go, meals left to eat, junque left to buy, stories left to collect. And I'm not over it.

## OPERATING INSTRUCTIONS

There are hot dogs and hot sauces herein. But this is not a guide to singular southern foods or where to find them at their very best. Rather, this is a handbook that examines some of the ways we've gotten where we're going: the signs that bait, the burgers that sate, the maps that guide, and the mixtapes that score the ride. As they do on the road, chains appear in these pages with frequency and tell particular stories of convenience, cost, and ambition. But there are also detours to spots out yonder and beelines to specific destinations—oftentimes a road trip's reason for being.

The approach is best summed up on one of South of the Border's towering billboards, which proclaims, "Roads' Scholar!" Combining interviews and articles, and many miles and meals, this book takes a serious look at the history of southern roads, whose role in connecting and modernizing the region cannot be understated, as well as many of the foods and accompanying objects along the way. But it does so by nodding at a billboard's brevity, with shorter entries that invite further reading, travel-ing, eating, and understanding.

## ABOUT THIS MANUAL

Covered at a clip, the mileage here is exhausting but not exhaustive.* Locations were chosen to accompany a specific idea, with an eye toward geographical breadth and range, including both southern and border states—and other places, too. After all, concepts travel as easily as col-onels, so southern fried chicken ends up in New York, and New York's "famous" hot dogs influence a cadre of "famous" stands and joints across the region.

* WARRANTY DOES NOT COVER OMISSIONS.

# ROAD SIDES

24 ↑
FEET
TALL
—
POKEABLE*
STYROFOAM
→

*ACTUAL POKING IS DISCOURAGED.

# ARCHITECTURE

Between Candor and Ellerbe, North Carolina, Lee and Amy Berry counted about forty-four produce stands along Highway 220 and knew they needed a way to differentiate their own. So in 2002 the Berrys built a berry—a twenty-four-foot-tall building shaped like the strawberries they sell. According to Lee, business immediately doubled.

Object-shaped structures (deemed "ducks" among architects, in reference to a duck-shaped building on Long Island) aren't all whimsy. As the Berrys' berry illustrates, they advertise, tempting motorists to the roadside. And they exalt, often celebrating something about a particular place or its people. There are earlier examples, including French draughtsman Jean-Jacques Lequeu's plans for a cow-like barn in the late eighteenth century, and James V. Lafferty's "Lucy," an elephant-shaped building south of Atlantic City that was built in 1881 and still stands near its original location. But novelty architecture found its giant footing in the 1920s along an expanding network of highways. "Rural farm silos became bottles selling automotive oil, and water towers could by the seeming touch of a wand become a pineapple or a strawberry," writes architectural historian David Gebhard.

About five miles north of Auburn, Alabama, John F. Williams constructed a wooden sixty-four-foot-tall soda bottle in 1924 to lure drivers taking the Florida Short Route—a road that cut quickly toward the Sunshine State. Known locally as "Chero-Cola" Williams for the sodas he bottled at his plant in nearby Opelika, he modeled the bottle after a bright orange Nehi. The Bottle (sometimes called the Twist Inn) housed a gas station and grocery, and underneath its cap, an observation deck once visited by FDR. It's plausible that a young Flannery O'Connor stopped at the site, too, or at least heard of it one state over in Georgia, as the Frosty Bottle she invented in *Wise Blood* is strikingly similar—"a hotdog stand in the shape of an Orange Crush with frost painted in blue around the top of it." Alabama's Bottle burned down in 1936, but it still shows up on maps to describe the community around Highways 147 and 280, and in 2015, a historical marker was erected to commemorate the building. (The first fifty folks to attend its ceremony were rewarded with a cold Nehi.)

Programmatic architecture took on new shapes with the introduction of new materials such as fiberglass, which became particularly popular after World War II. Across Florida, it formed a fleet of Twistee Treat buildings in the 1980s that resembled soft-serve cones. And in the town of Kissimmee, it crowned Orange World with a citrus dome. Envisioned by Eli Sfassie, and referred to as "Eli's Folly" because it took apparently the original builders so long to construct, the oversized orange had to be finished in the late 1980s by ironworkers whom Sfassie met in a Waffle House next door to his store, just a short drive from Disneyworld. That theme park is home to an extensive set of novelty buildings, most designed by

world-renowned architects, including Michael Graves. But more often than not, "ducks" are conceived or constructed by novice builders.

In Ellerbe, Lee Berry was stumped when his wife Amy suggested they create the enormous strawberry. But two hours later, he says, he'd sketched an octagonal building that he planned to cover in spray foam. Kids occasionally poke holes in the exterior that have to be patched, and it's repainted almost every year, but otherwise the berry has held up—even withstanding a move when a highway expansion project demanded its relocation in 2011. For that, Berry says he phoned the guy who transported the Cape Hatteras Lighthouse nearly three thousand feet along North Carolina's coast—figuring it best to keep his focus on the roadside and let someone else handle business on the actual road.

## HILLS OF SNOW

### SMITHFIELD, NORTH CAROLINA

A silver lining of my parents' divorce was that my dad moved into an apartment, and, not long after, town royalty moved into the unit next door. Or so they seemed to me. The Hill family owned Hills of Snow, a snow cone–shaped building in the center of Smithfield, North Carolina, that was the crux of all of our eight-year-old dreams.

Originally envisioned as Snow World, the snow-cone stand was built in 1984 by Tom Hill, who formed the base out of wood and the snowy cap out of a thick foam he painted blue. Hill then settled upon a play on his last name, fashioning its double Ls into straws that jut from the snowcapped roof. "My mom always said that he dreamed up the design and made it a reality," says Kristy Hill Hinnant, the late Hill's daughter.

The idea came to him during a stretch in New Orleans, where he'd gone to join his uncle in the used-car business. "He went to do cars but got into chicken," says Hinnant. While frying birds in the city for some five years,

Hill noticed there was often a snowball place next to a chicken shack. So when he moved back to North Carolina, he created the same: the Chicken Barn, with a drumstick protruding from its sign, and across the parking lot, his architectural triumph, Hills of Snow.

From his time in New Orleans, Hill mastered the city's fluffy take on snowballs—a style originally created by hand-shaving ice that hardly resembles what's in the more prevalent ice-chipped cones sold as "sno" in other places. The process was simplified in the 1930s, when George Ortolano and Ernest Hansen separately created electric machines that produce something akin to real powdery snow. But to get it right, the shaving process still required some finesse. "There's a way of doing it that makes it lighter," says Hinnant, who learned the technique from her dad. "The snow is everything. You want it to melt on your tongue."

Hinnant also learned how to make her father's syrups—101 flavors of "pure enjoyment" that are mixed across the parking lot in a building called the Sugar Shack. "His syrup, his ice, his everything," Hinnant says. "I keep everything the same." And it still feels very much the same to me. As a result, I can recite most of the menu's 101 flavors from memory. Still, each time I step onto Hills of Snow's wooden platform to place my order, I stare at the menu, thinking maybe it's the day I'll go for something new. There's a childlike temptation in a list that includes Tiger's Blood, Tutti Frutti, and Vanilla Snow Cream. But there's also a lifetime of the same choice, which never disappoints. It's been Wild Strawberry for as long as I can remember, handed through the snow-cone window in a Styrofoam cup and accompanied by the short phrase Mr. Hill made the standard: "Enjoy."

# B

## BILLBOARDS

The Nahunta Pork Center proclaims itself "America's Largest Pork Display," referring to its extensive inventory of bacon, ham, and sausage—some forty fresh cuts of meat. But the superlative could just as easily refer to the company's bevy of yellow billboards. With their grinning, crown-adorned hogs, the signs tower over a stretch of US Highway 70 in Eastern North Carolina, appearing every few miles.

Repetition has been common practice for billboards since this form of marketing began. So aggressive were the advertisers who hung posters around Pittsburgh in the early 1890s, the inaugural issue of *Billboard Advertising* claimed a bill sticker had plastered an ad to "the carcass of a horse while the body was still warm." Describing the folks who hung bills around New York, the magazine reported how competing admen covered and re-covered each other's bills with such zeal that the city's papered street barrels appeared bloated, as if they "were wearing extremely pronounced crinoline." These stories are not the music journalism for which *Billboard* magazine is known today. But they were as closely followed, shedding light on the era's contentious postering wars, as well as on the musical and theatrical productions the posters often announced. (Measuring around fifty square feet, the first large-scale bill advertised a circus in 1835.)

With no regulations in place, early advertisers used every rock, barn, building, barrel, horse, and hilltop they could paint or plaster with a sales

pitch. As Sam Houghteling, cofounder of the first national sign-painting business, bragged about work he began in the 1870s, "I've painted on rocks while standing up to my neck in water . . . and put the name of 'Vitality Bitters' on Lookout Mountain." Beginning in the 1930s, the Southern dvertising Company continued this style of branding to market an outcrop of Lookout, which afforded a panoramic view of seven states and other mountainous formations, stenciling "See Rock City" on tin roofs across the United States.

Responding to an onslaught of renegade ads that were painted and plastered across the landscape, various organizations formed in the late 1800s to create and enforce standard practices, including what would become the Outdoor Advertising Association of America. By 1900, the industry was becoming streamlined with the introduction of a uniform billboard structure that attracted mass-produced campaigns by the likes of Coca-Cola. Such companies took to heart the Outdoor Advertising Agency

assessment in the early 1920s that "the highway has become the buyway," a means to literally drive the market toward specific products and places. But not everyone bought into it, as billboards cluttered the roadside and obscured trees and vistas with branded content. "Public feeling is going to bring about regulation so you don't have a solid diet of billboards on all the roads," Lady Bird Johnson, an outspoken opponent, told reporters. In 1965, her efforts helped pass the Highway Beautification Act, which placed regulations on the placement and size of billboards, though not on their content, which is at turns informative, entertaining, and offensive.

Billboards for South of the Border, Alan Schafer's sprawling tourist trap off I-95 in South Carolina, have long been criticized for the park's mascot, a Hispanic cartoon caricature named Pedro, who is often printed alongside misspellings to convey his supposed accent ("WHEN YOU'RE HOT, YOU'RE HOT! COOL EET WEETH PEDRO!"). More recently, Lowes Foods, a grocery chain headquartered in North Carolina, annoyed prudish drivers with signs that paired suggestive clumps of fruit with sayings such as "GROCERY FINALLY GROWS A PEAR." But perhaps more central to billboard debates are advertisements by alcohol and tobacco companies, as well as those by religious groups, who use the space to make proclamations. In the late '90s, an anonymous donor commissioned a Florida ad agency to create billboards that displayed pithy sayings attributed to God. The campaign was picked up by an office of the OAAA and advertised by members on hundreds of boards nationwide with quotations like, "Need Directions?—God."

On the road, it's about being concise and memorable, providing an image or message that lingers well past the initial sighting. In 2010, Bloom, another North Carolina grocer, stretched the limits, erecting a billboard that emitted the scent of pepper and charcoal around a fifty-foot-radius during rush hour each day to market a particular brand of steak. Understandably, they were grilled for it.

# SOUTH OF THE BORDER

## HAMER, SOUTH CAROLINA

Standing under the brim of Pedro's two-hundred-foot Sombrero Observation Tower, we survey the three hundred acres around us—a fake Mexican border town populated by a ramshackle herd of neon animal statues and weary tourists. This place is said to be home to a cult favorite, Blenheim Ginger Ale, which my friend and I have come to write about and photograph. But though we find stacks of the sodas sold in gift shops like Mexico East, nothing at South of the Border announces that the drinks are brewed and bottled on-site. It's a conspicuous omission for a place that is known for its outlandish self-promotion. SOB is emblazoned on hundreds of trinkets, including snow globes, shirts, ashtrays, and magnets, as well as on countless billboards that stretch from Florida to New Jersey along I-95.

Located just below the North Carolina line, South of the Border began in 1949 as a beer stand that catered to thirsty folks in Robeson County, where the sale of alcohol was then prohibited. But the park expanded its footprint and its offerings significantly in the following decades, especially with the construction of I-95, adding a gas station, motels, a miniature golf course, multiple restaurants and gift shops, and a fireworks stand. To entice travelers off the road, founder Alan Schafer commissioned giant neon sculptures and, for better or worse, memorable billboards, going so far as to establish a design group, the Ace-Hi, to create the signs. "I keep a legal pad and three or four felt-tip pens by the bed at night," he once told a journalist, "and very often I wake up at three or four o'clock in the morning and get an idea in my head—like a great billboard."

Schafer's ideas included copious puns such as "CHILI TODAY—HOT TAMALE," or "YOU'VE NEVER SAUSAGE A PLACE!" But there were also

those whose language and imagery were less playful, including a billboard with a Native American caricature that read,
"Don't be lost injun! Get a Reservation." (Neighboring counties
are home to members of the Lumbee tribe, North Carolina's
largest Native population.) There's also the matter of Pedro, the
stereotypical Hispanic man who wears a serape and sombrero
and appears on every SOB billboard as a heavily accented
spokesman for the park.

    Schafer seemingly thrived on conflict and contradic-
tions. As scholar Nicole King describes in *Sombreros and
Motorcycles in a Newer South*, South of the Border is "both
controversial and family-friendly." It's been progressive, supposedly opening its motel doors to all races in 1954 ("we checked
only the color of their money, not their skins," Schafer reportedly said), a move that incited the KKK to ride through
the park several times issuing threats. And it's also been
extremely regressive: in the 1960s, Schafer opened
Confederateland, U.S.A., hawking Confederate memorabilia, as well as Pedro's Plantation, where cotton
was available for picking. (Both operations
have since closed.) Rides and games

for children also operated not far from the Dirty Old Man's Shop (a soft-core porn store that's since closed, too) and the Silver Slipper Arcade (accused of issuing illegal payouts from video gambling machines). It's not hard to understand why my mother and my friends' mothers were inclined to speed past the park.

I visited for the first time when I was eighteen. On a road trip after high school graduation, my friends and I pulled into the expansive parking lot and took an elevator to the top of the sombrero tower, where we walked around the observation brim. As a group of younger kids fidgeted with firecrackers, I wished we'd heeded our parents' warnings. But some twenty years later, I've made at least twenty more stops—sifting through the souvenirs, taking snapshots of SOB's neon beasts, and loading up on six-packs of spicy Blenheim ales.

On our reporting trip, my friend Kate and I eventually locate the Blenheim soda factory on the property's edge, tucked behind the SOBMX motocross track. The mustard-yellow building is nondescript, dull in comparison to most of SOB's architecture. But the stuff made inside is clearly of this place. Ales labeled regular are sometimes fiery hot, while those marked hot are sometimes mild—thoroughly unpredictable.

# C

# CARS

For more than fifty years, John W. Raiford reportedly packed four ornate hats to take to work at Atlanta's Varsity drive-in. They were covered in long ribbons and flowing bandanas, and adorned with plastic spice containers and pill bottles that were tied on with neckties or string. "The for-

mer manager advised me when I first came here to get a gimmick to entertain the customers," Raiford told the *LA Times* about the job he held for more than fifty years. "The next day I made a hat." Raiford, better known by his nickname Flossie Mae, had good reason to want to stand out. By the 1950s, the Varsity had christened itself the "World's Largest Drive-In," employing around 150 carhops, who would jump onto a car's running board to take orders, asking, "What'll ya have?"

Canopied drive-ins like the Varsity in Atlanta, Shoney's in West Virginia, or the Pig Stand in Texas were immensely popular destinations after World War II, catering to an increasingly mobile public. Though the Varsity was capable of seating a hundred people inside its dining room,

← STASHBOARD!

# THE DASHBOARD

PLUS— COMPARTMENTS FOR CAR CRAVINGS

---

| | |
|---|---|
| **DASHBOARD** | SHELF FOR SANDWICHES |
| **GLOVEBOX** | CABINET FOR CRACKERS |
| **CONSOLE** | CUPBOARD FOR CHIPS |
| **DOOR POCKET** | STASH FOR SODAS |
| **CUP HOLDER** | CACHE FOR CANDY |
| **FLOORBOARD** | RECEPTACLE FOR WRAPPERS |

the focus was outside, where two hundred cars parked for a menu of hot dogs, hamburgers, and fried hand pies, and, equally important, a lively scene that emphasized being seen. As scholars John A. Jakle and Keith A. Sculle wrote, "The drive-in was fully symbolic of its time—an era of rapidly growing automobile dependence and thus an era when owning and using cars came to carry profound social and personal meaning."

Introduced to the United States from Germany in the early 1890s, cars originally functioned as toys for the rich, who jaunted joyfully in them down country roads. Then, in 1908, Henry Ford debuted the Model T, an automobile whose assembly-line production made it an affordable option for millions of Americans. In less than ten years, the car's price tag dropped from $825 to just over $300. And though the Depression temporarily slowed the growth of car culture, it was booming once again by the 1950s. In 1955, it's reported that sixty million people owned cars, up from eight million in the early 1920s. One famously smitten owner was the author E. B. White, who called the Model T "the miracle God had wrought."

Though miraculous in its way, the car was far from perfect—which, for some, was part of the fun. "When you bought a Ford, you figured you had a start—a vibrant, spirited framework to which could be screwed an almost limitless assortment of decorative and functional hardware," White wrote in the *New Yorker*. "A Ford was born naked as a baby, and a flourishing industry grew up out of correcting its rare deficiencies and combating its fascinating diseases." Part of the new market included fixes for hungry and thirsty travelers. There was the Lincoln Kitchenette, a metal cabinet that affixed to the running board and could hold up to twenty-five pounds of ice, and the "snack tray," which dangled from the dashboard, kept drinks upright, and included a shelf for sandwiches. The now-ubiquitous sunken plastic cup holder didn't debut until 1983, with the Dodge minivan.

Today, with around 276 million registered vehicles in the United States and amid dire concerns about carbon emissions and climate change, advances have more to do with removing cars from the road or making them more green. It's estimated that individual car ownership will reach its peak by 2020, then decrease quickly in favor of shared rides and supposedly more efficient self-driving cars. It's unclear what such shifts would mean, though E. B. White's take on the Model T seems apt: "Flourishing industries rose and fell with it."

## KING TUT DRIVE-IN
### BECKLEY, WEST VIRGINIA

We came for the hot dogs and found them aplenty in West Virginia. But there's also, surprisingly, a remarkable number of drive-ins across the state. My friend, a fellow folklorist also named Emily Elizabeth, pulls her car under King Tut's canopy in Beckley, marking our third such stop of the day. She flashes her lights and a carhop appears shortly after to take our order—a hot dog on a toasted English bun topped with the state's

A SILVER PLATTER ↳ FIT FOR A KING ↳

essential combo of chili, slaw, mustard, and onions. It's somewhere around our seventh dog of the afternoon, so when it arrives on a metal tray that latches to the window, Emily, ever the Girl Scout, slices the serving in half with a pocketknife. Three bites each and we're off, curving back toward Charleston to continue our research.

Dave McKay embarked on a similar research trip more than sixty years ago when his mother took the family to Charleston to eat at the first Shoney's. A few years later, in 1955, his father, John, made an offer on a drive-in of his own, propositioning the Tutweiler family, owners of King Tut. "Part of the deal," says McKay, "was that he had to give [Mr. Tutweiler] a free chicken dinner every Sunday." Mr. Tutweiler showed up for his end of the bargain. "Every damn Sunday," McKay laughs.

In contrast to Beckley's other two drive-ins at the time—Pete & Bob's and Phil's, which primarily focused on quick hot dogs and hamburgers—John McKay also offered slow-cooked dinners, including pan-fried chicken livers, brown beans, and pies. He relied on recipes that his mother, Kenneth, collected over her impressive career overseeing the dining rooms at Higbee's in Cleveland and Schrafft's in New York, and also drew upon what he found at trade shows; John McKay had spent the first part of his career as a route salesman for Sexton Quality Foods (now US Foods). "He introduced pizza to Beckley in 1955," says Dave McKay, who has run the restaurant since he retired from AT&T in 2004. Now in his seventies, he lives in Georgia but travels to West Virginia once a month to spend time at Tut's and visit with the regulars. He guesses three-fourths of these folks are third-generation customers.

"Things don't change as fast here as other places," says McKay, referencing West Virginia's notable number of drive-ins, which have remained long past the genre's peak in the 1950s and '60s. It's a joke, but I'm glad that in the case of Tut's, McKay's statement seems true. A year later, on a different writing trip, I pull under the canopy with another folklorist friend and flash my headlights. The service is still quick, and the homemade menu still expansive. But this time, I order much more than one hot dog.

# DIRECTIONS

"WILL YOU PLEASE TELL ME IF THERE IS AN AUTO
ROAD FROM CHATTANOOGA AND CORINTH, MISSISSIPPI?
I KNOW THE ROAD FROM CHATTANOOGA VIA NASHVILLE
TO MEMPHIS, AND IT IS NO GOOD UNLESS YOU
TRAVEL IT IN A FLYING MACHINE."

— DIXIE HIGHWAY MAGAZINE

Early roads were ill marked and often shoddy, muddy paths that were hardly maintained in the South. So columns like *Dixie Highway* magazine's "Touring Queries" and guides including the *Official Automobile Blue Book* sprang up to offer directions. Advertised as the "veritable motorist's encyclopedia," the *Blue Book* paired hand-drawn roadmaps with turn-by-turn text to direct a driver's every move, recommending hotels and roadside attractions and warning about perilous curves or inclines. "Heed them," the guide instructed of such cautions. "They may save your life or the lives of others." But what the *Blue Book* and others like it didn't caution against were the humiliating and life-threatening obstacles nonwhite travelers faced on the road, including sundown towns in the Jim Crow

South and unwelcoming restaurants or service stations all over. In response, Victor Hugo Green launched the *Negro Motorist Green Book* in 1936.

Building on the knowledge and contacts Green had gathered as a postal worker in Harlem, the initial *Green Book* published addresses for diners, motels, car garages, barbershops, liquor stores, private homes—any place that welcomed people of color traveling in the greater New York area. Over a third of the restaurants in the 1937 edition offered southern or "country" dishes, such as the "Southern Home Cooking" at Major's Lunch Room or the "Finest Liquors and Southern Cooking" at the Butterly Inn, located across the street

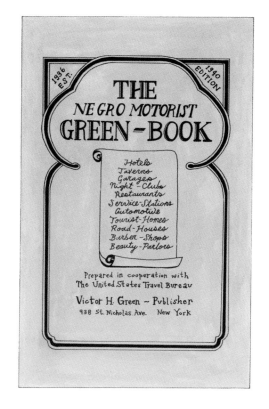

from each other in Tuckahoe, New York. But as civil rights leader Julian Bond once noted, "It was a guidebook that told you not where the best places were to eat, but where there was any place."

In this, the *Green Book* was vastly different from *Adventures in Good Eating*, a compilation by Kentucky's Duncan Hines (later of boxed cake fame), which also launched in 1936. For that book, Hines, a former traveling salesman, selected the finest establishments, in his opinion, in all fifty states. "On a pleasure trip—particularly in strange localities—it is important to take no chances," Hines wrote in a 1945 printing. "Nearly everyone wants at least one outstanding meal a day." With its own intent to "take no chances," the *Green Book* expanded its coverage of welcoming establishments beyond New York. By 1938, it addressed all points east of the

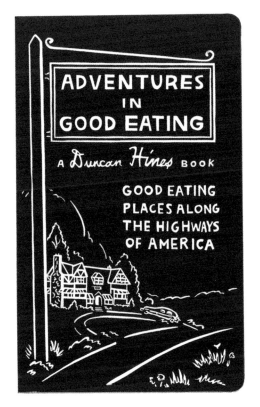

Mississippi. And by 1963, it listed venues in places as distant as Canada, the Caribbean, Latin America, Europe, and Africa. But following the Civil Rights Act of 1964, which abolished segregation in public spaces, demand for the *Green Book* waned. It ceased publication with its 1966–1967 edition, disappearing from shelves in Esso gas stations, one of the major outlets that had sold them for a dollar.

What remained was Esso's own line of foldable maps, given away for free. Like those from Shell, Gulf, and other oil companies, they contained an intricate network of numbered highways and easy-to-read symbols like the red, white, and blue interstate shield fashioned by Richard Oliver, a traffic engineer in the Texas Highway Department, who won a contest with his design in 1957. Oliver told a local paper he felt the shape and colors signaled federal authority.

On *The Great NC BBQ Map*, the interstate shield ranks low on the legend, listed below symbols that designate a joint's particulars: whole hog barbecue versus part of a pig, vinegar-based sauce versus tomato-spiked versions, and so on. Like its offshoot, *The Great Carolina Fried Chicken Map*, the barbecue guide is part of a growing collection of niche or collectible maps—print and digital—that catalog a single dish or cuisine and that offer guidance for every fork in the road.

# FLORIDA WELCOME CENTERS

## MULTIPLE LOCATIONS IN FLORIDA

Surrounded by kitschy memorabilia in the Visit Florida headquarters and rattling off Florida facts and stories, David Dodd practically emanates the state's sunshine feel. "Tourism is a funny thing," he says of his twenty-six-year career in the industry. "It's one of the best businesses. And it's fun." Overseeing the state's five Welcome Centers as Vice President of Visitor Services sounds stressful to me. They're the places where thousands of road-weary travelers pull in looking for directions and advice each day. But Dodd assures me that "nine out of ten people coming in those doors are in a good mood. They've planned this. They're excited." And if not, a small cup of juice helps tip them over.

Along with 900,000 maps and 14 million brochures, Welcome Centers hand out six swimming pools worth of 100 percent Florida orange and grapefruit juices each year, as they've done since the beginning, and all for free. The first Florida Welcome Center—then called a Welcome Station—opened in Yulee (near Jacksonville) in 1949, one of the first of its kind in the nation. "It was a big deal," says Vivian Armstrong, whose father was commissioner of Nassau County. "I was there, ten years old, just having a good time, drinking orange juice, and running across the road." Armstrong grew up to have a thirty-plus year career at the Welcome Center. Located off major interstate entrances to Florida, the centers provide good jobs in what are mostly rural areas. For that reason, Dodd says employees "tend to stay on," racking up decades of service—and knowledge.

Prospective attendants must pass a 167-question test, which covers topics like Florida history, geography, government relations, and tourism. "My first day on the job I looked at all of those brochures and was told that

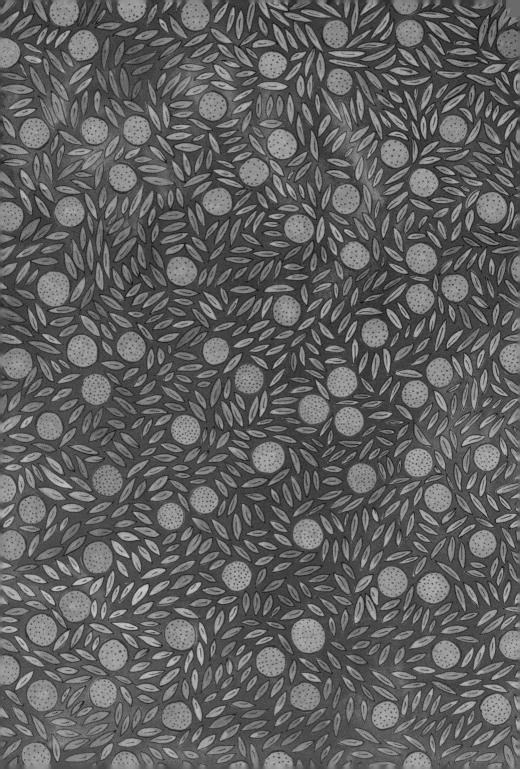

I had to know what was in every one of them and I thought, 'No way!'" Paulette Anderson recalled in an interview. "Then when they told me I had to read the map upside down, I looked at them like, 'What have I got myself into?'"

After just six months on the job, Patricia Brown wound up in the psych ward of the South Georgia Medical Center. "They thought I had absolutely lost my brains," she later said. "Really I had just never seen so many people. . . . It bombarded me." On her first day (she went on to a near-forty-year career), Brown estimates that ten thousand people walked in the door needing way more than just directions.

"Where can I take a dog on the beach? Where can I wear a thong on the beach? Where can I pick an orange?" Dodd lists typical questions, including the frequent "Where can I see an alligator?" "We're all about customer service," he emphasizes. "You can get a brochure or map anywhere."

THERE'S AMAZING INSIDE

FLORIDA
ORANGE JUICE ®

# ENTERTAINMENT

Before bed each night, Randy Koplin wandered between giant dinosaur legs and wished a Sphinx sweet dreams. His family's house was situated on the edge of a miniature golf course on Florida's Miracle Strip, where his father Lee perfected the art of constructing giant cement sculptures in the late 1950s. Located across the street from the Panama City Beach pier, Goofy Golf's towering monkey and wide-mouthed fish invited tourists—especially kids and their parents—over for an hour of sport and strange sightseeing with the explicit goal of having fun.

It was the height of roadside prosperity, and all that was weird or wonderful was there to entertain—and, for locals, to make money. As historian Tracy J. Revels puts it in *Sunshine Paradise*, "Anyone with a collection of American Indian artifacts, a large garden, or an exotic animal could put up a billboard and charge admission." In Iowa, George Kern reportedly lured visitors to his country store with little more than the promise of a petrified ham. And as an attraction in Florida, residents marketed droopy, pod-filled *Kigelia africana* plants as bountiful "sausage trees." Across the Sunshine State, mom-and-pop road stops became so abundant that the Florida Attractions Association formed in 1949 to offer legitimacy, placing FAA emblems at approved venues.

Like Koplin's alien Cyclops at Goofy Golf, Florida's attractions could seem otherworldly. But they were grounded in a tradition of tourism and self-promotion that included St. Augustine's health spas of the late 1800s and Jacksonville's early amusement parks, including the Ostrich Farm, which began racing birds for spectacle in 1898. Overwhelmingly, these parks operated as whites-only venues, sometimes hosting so-called Jim Crow Days. As scholar Lauren Rabinovitz details in *Electric Dreamland*, African American residents in the North and South responded by establishing black-owned entertainment centers, like Jacksonville's Lincoln Park, "ensur[ing they] were not excluded from the form of urban leisure that was being ushered in by modernity." Similar to white parks, black venues were also often located at the end of public transit lines and featured the latest rides, games, and concessions.

SAUSAGE TREE

The national appeal for amusement only increased after World War II, when Americans found themselves with more free time and money. For many, the idea of vacations became an entrenched part of the American Dream, as did, in October 1971, a certain mouse. In Orlando, Disney World harnessed the celebrity of its characters to become the ultimate all-in-one vacation spot. For an average of $33 a day, a family of four could do it all—smile with Snow White, twirl in one of the Mad Hatter's spinning cups, and down a couple of ice cream cones. And they could do it all year round. Walt Disney chose Florida to house the offshoot of his California park because of its temperate climate, as well as its accessibility by car (the construction of new roads made this even more of a reality). In addition, it was home to undeveloped swaths of land—enough room to build Cinderella's castle.

ORIGINAL MICKEY BAR— INTRODUCED IN THE '80s

DISNEY'S MOST POPULAR TREAT

Disney's West and East Coast parks inspired several southerners to expand their visions, or to create something new entirely. In Arlington, Texas, Angus Wynne founded Six Flags in 1961, with the belief that regional parks would be more accessible and affordable for Texans wishing to be entertained. The first spin-off was Six Flags Over Georgia in 1967. And in the Tennessee mountains, Dolly Parton also dreamt of creating something with local appeal. "I've always joked that I want to be a female Walt Disney," Parton once said of the inspiration for Dollywood. "In my early days, I thought if I do get successful, I want to come back here and build something special to honor my parents and my people." In addition to offering concessions and rides, Dollywood promotes traditional Appalachian music and crafts.

Still, Florida leads the way with attractions, counting some of America's largest and most popular parks—Busch Gardens, SeaWorld, Legoland, and Universal Orlando—among them. As singular destinations shaped by big budgets, such venues helped usher out many of the early roadside stops, which were more often happened upon on meandering drives. Also contributing to the demise of smaller places was the growth of interstate highways, which passed them by entirely. Those that remain, Revels argues, are still splendid. Across Florida, the jagged-tooth entryway to Gatorland, the teeming Citrus Tower with its panoramic view, and the Sphinx on the strip at Goofy Golf endure as incentives to pull over. And they still entertain.

## WEEKI WACHEE SPRINGS

### WEEKI WACHEE, FLORIDA

As I step out of the air-conditioned snack bar at Weeki Wachee Springs, the Florida heat fogs my glasses. The high is 91, the humidity even higher. But when I find Victoria Cox at the edge of Buccaneer Bay, a crystal blue swimming hole, she's shivering in a navy sweat suit, MERMAID printed in white letters across her chest and thigh.

Thirty minutes earlier, Cox was performing in a sequined top and Lycra tail some sixteen feet below the surface as one of the sisters in Hans Christian Andersen's *The Little Mermaid*. It was admittedly a bit cheesy. A blue satin curtain lifted to reveal young women (plus one man and a costumed sea turtle, the beloved Chester) lip-synching to steel-drum tunes in an underwater theater carved into the spring's limestone walls. But the routine was nothing short of impressive—the synchronized swimming, the wrangling of air hoses for breathing, the eyes wide open with no goggles, the fish and manatees that sometimes swim into the "stage," and the current that runs a swift five miles per hour. For Cox, the challenge is

diving into the 74-degree water. "You really have to love the job because you'll freeze your butt off," she says.

Weeki Wachee is one of the deepest natural springs in the nation—a network of caverns where rock bottom has reportedly never been reached. Newton Perry, who trained the elite Navy frogmen (a precursor to the SEALs) to work underwater in World War II, staked out the overgrown spot in 1946 as a potential tourist site. Having developed a canister-less oxygen hose that divers didn't have to strap on their backs, he moved on to recruiting young women to swim and dance in the cool water. The first show opened to an eighteen-seat theater in 1947. To attract visitors, the mermaids stood in their bathing suits along US 19, waved down cars, and then dove into the spring to do their twirls and tricks. A classic, which is still performed, involves eating a banana and having a drink underwater—originally Arkansas's Grapette soda, its bright plum hue easily visible to onlookers in the theater. (Today, the mermaids drink colored water in plastic Coke bottles as part of their performance.)

In 1959, the American Broadcasting Company bought Weeki Wachee's theater, bolstering the show's theatrics and constructing the current four-hundred-seat space. And in 2008, Weeki Wachee became an official Florida-owned park, meaning mermaids are now state employees. Women travel from all over to audition, including Cox, who drove three times from North Carolina to Florida to try out before finally snagging the job. "Basically, it was the universe telling me I had to graduate college first," she says.

Cox uses her degree in costume design from the University of North Carolina School of the Arts to make crowns and tails. Her goal is to one day open a mermaid school—one that will be about more than entertainment. The idea is that children relate to mermaids more easily than they do to water-related issues like sea-level rise or sustainable seafood. At

Weeki Wachee, they clap and sing along, mesmerized by the underwater swimmers.

"We're not like other women fighting traffic on the shore," the mermaids sing in one number, "tired of going shopping, living lives that are a bore." Cox puts it differently while finishing her lunch between shows. "I don't just want to be a pretty face or a Barbie," she says. "I want to do something."

CONTAINS 6 OZ.

*Grapette* SODA

IMITATION GRAPE FLAVOR

← THE MEAL OF MERMAIDS* ↘

*CONSUME UNDER WATER

# F

## FIXINS

PETE & RE-PETE ↙

The Hot Texas Weiner is deep fried not in the Lone Star State but in Jersey, where it's been bedecked with spicy mustard, onions, and a beanless chili since the 1920s. Another misnomer is West Virginia's Slaw Dog (a hot dog with slaw *and* chili), which contrasts with its Chili Bun (no dog, just chili on a bun). But deconstructed, most hot dogs are as good as a Plott Hound at following a trail home. From a finely chopped cabbage to a long-stewed chili, a weenie's fixins say something about the people or places that made them.

In Birmingham, Alabama, Greek-owned joints like Gus's Hot Dogs are known for a tart and spicy sauce that's served alongside mustard, kraut, and onions and that dates back to the early twentieth century, when Theodore Gulas first served it at his twenty-by-seven-foot hot dog stand on Second Avenue North. "It ain't chili," Gus Koutroulakis of Pete's Famous Hot Dogs (RIP) once told the Southern Foodways Alliance. "It's just a regular sauce." When pressed, Koutroulakis wouldn't name the ingredients, but quietly counted about fifteen to himself (vinegar, ketchup, chili powder, and allspice likely among them).

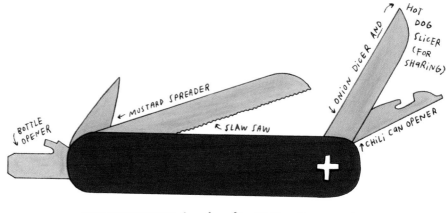

BOTTLE OPENER
← MUSTARD SPREADER
← SLAW SAW
↙ ONION DICER AND
HOT DOG SLICER (FOR SHARING)
↑ CHILI CAN OPENER

## )ALL-IN-ONE( WV HOT DOG PREPAREDNESS KIT

In a swath of central and south West Virginia, it's a slaw dog that marks the territory. Some, like the state's folklorist Emily Hilliard, have called the supposed Slaw Line, which divides the state's preferred fix-ins, a "Mason–Dixon of condiments." Coleslaw credit is often given to the Stopette Drive-In (also RIP) in Charleston, West Virginia, where the topping was being served as early as 1922. But the exact origins of the slaw dog are unclear. As Hilliard has argued, it's likely due to the many perks of cabbage, which is cheap, hardy, and well suited as a backyard crop to the cool hills of Appalachia.

The condiment caught on. According to barbecue historian John Shelton Reed, coleslaw's Dutch and German cousin *Krautsalat* hitched a ride on the Great Wagon Road, making its way from Pennsylvania and West Virginia down to North Carolina. There, served atop a barbecue sandwich or a Carolina-style hot dog (with chili, mustard, and onions), variations of the slaw itself act as a compass, pinpointing a specific region of the state. Finely chopped cabbage spiked with vinegar and a dash of ketchup means the Piedmont. And mayonnaise-based slaw denotes eastern North Carolina, where it provides a cool counterpart to spicy vinegar-based barbecue sauce or, as it's done at Raleigh's Roast Grill, hot dogs peppered with a dash of Texas Pete. That hot sauce, like the Hot Texas Weiner, confuses with its name, as it aims to associate itself with the Lone Star State's penchant for heat. But to folks in North Carolina, where Texas Pete is made, the moniker hardly matters. It's the ingredients—peppers and vinegar—that signal home.

## SING WONG RESTAURANT

### PORTSMOUTH, VIRGINIA

From behind what looks like an old bank teller window, a woman we recognize as Patsy Wong gives us something of a side-eye when we order two boxes of yock-a-mein. "Do y'all know what that is?" she asks, and we all nod, though even the Norfolk native in our group has never tasted it. "OK, just checking," she says, turning toward the kitchen. "Just checking."

At its most basic, Virginia's yock-a-mein (sometimes called yock or yaket) refers to a takeout box of lo mein noodles. Once plentiful in African American neighborhoods in the Tidewater—a swath of southeastern Virginia that encompasses Norfolk, Suffolk, and Portsmouth—the dish was likely brought to the region by Chinese immigrants in the early twentieth century and combines Chinese and soul food traditions. Tidewater yock differs from New Orleans's ya-ka-mein, which commonly consists of spaghetti noodles in a murky broth. But it's similar in that it's fairly cheap and simple, often providing fuel for late nights (in New Orleans it sometimes goes by the nickname "Old Sober").

"You're just cooking noodles," Wong once told oral historian Sara Wood. "There's no recipes, no measuring it right. I mean, there's no ingredients." A box of yock is all about the fixins. To the lo mein noodles, which are made in a Tidewater factory, a base of ketchup is added, though sometimes it's brown gravy or broth. Then there's a choice of meat: boiled chicken or pork, sautéed shrimp or beef, or, at Sing Wong Restaurant, hot Philadelphia sausages. To top things off, there are the options of chopped white onions or a hard-boiled egg. And for the finish, there's soy sauce, apple cider vinegar, and cayenne pepper to taste. "It's up to the customer to use what they want or what they like," Wong has said. "It's just plain unless you count the ketchup as a seasoning."

Sing Wong Restaurant wasn't the first place to dish out boxes of yock, which appeared on area menus at least as far back as the 1920s. In fact, when Sing and Mee Sau Wong opened their spot on Portsmouth's High Street in 1965, shortly after they immigrated to the United States from China, they sold mostly hamburgers, hot dogs, and fish sandwiches. But as fast food restaurants became more prevalent, the Wongs started offering cheaper dishes to compete, including yock, once under $2 a box.

Patsy's husband, Haymond, was fifteen when he moved to the states from China and began picking up shifts in his grandparents' restaurant. Now he's one of the Tidewater's last yock purveyors, as the owners of similar restaurants like Far East and Sun Wah have retired. The Wongs, who work alone, have said they have plans to retire soon, too.

Until then, Patsy oversees the front of the house, a small wood-paneled room that's covered in graffiti. Typical of the Tidewater, the décor consists mostly of posters for the US Navy, which accounts for a large part of the local economy. A far wall is covered in menus—one labeled CHINESE FOOD, with chop suey and yaket mein, another AMERICAN FOOD, featuring liver rice and a pork chop.

Haymond cooks the dishes in back, perceptible only by an occasional clang or low mumble. On Saturday night, he calls out to Patsy, who ducks back to the kitchen to retrieve our order. She motions to us, then slides the boxes of yock through the window along with bottles of soy, vinegar,

2016

Charlotte W.

Tony ♥

19>2 MOε 2017   MAPLE

757 to 404
DANIELE   6/9/17
WAS HERE
ALL THE WAY
FROM FL

6/14/12
"chie wuz"
here w/ the
"GiRLS"

4-27-10
Bayoon
repin
P.town

Carrie
Baker

LAZE
#1

JADA

A & A

Puff
wuz
Hea

J. EURε
#23

Kilan
&
Jay

D.T.P. 032
ב2ר-ב
032

VIP

"2015"

RUBICK

WARD
WiLLiAMS

EEW
LAA

Robert
♥
Beverly

Jameca
-n-
Duce
-n-
tha lil one
De'Angelo

Bek A.
was here

Treasure
-4-
Doug #16

Buck
m

yohyoh☺

LARRY
'O'

Land ♥

CRIMEY
TUNES

Bus
& ash ♥

yep   Brittany
waz
hea

Da Way!!

#sitdown

5AM

what
It is

♥
MHW

MARgUaZia

LOVES

A.T. N-Viaw

yep

Monique
8-31-83

JERRY
♥
J'NEITE

KaRiZma

streetfella

TRINA
L.O.4 Life

R.I.P.
LiTTLE
MAN
South
SiDE
KiNG

PERcY

ends :)

Matt O.

Newark
New Jersey
in da Buildin

◇MYRA KAY◇

IDA -13

CASEY

and hot pepper. "Just use a touch of vinegar," she instructs, and my friend Katy adds the fixins. Later, across town, we pop open the paper containers and stir everything together before digging in. Our results are good but admittedly plain—a combination we vow to top with a heavier hand another time.

# G

## GAS

Backed up by two men from the Shell Oil Company and equipped with a battery of guns, Harland Sanders went to see about a sign. It was the early 1930s and gas stations were something of a new frontier as early roads like the Dixie Highway pushed through rural communities including Corbin, Kentucky. Sanders had heard that a rival gas station owner was stenciling Standard Oil over one of his own advertisements—again!—so a shootout ensued. One of the Shell reps was killed and the other three men were arrested. But Sanders had secured his spot along Highway 25: a gas station in which he'd begin Kentucky Fried Chicken.

Pumping fuel and patting out biscuits, the Sanders Café and Service Station became a clever catchall for motorists in the manner of a modern day Buc-ee's; it even boasted a motel. Prior to the first gas station in 1905, drivers carried along everything they might need, loading fuel cans, tires, batteries, and at least a day's worth of food into their automobiles. Later, even when filling stations became more prevalent, their refreshments still

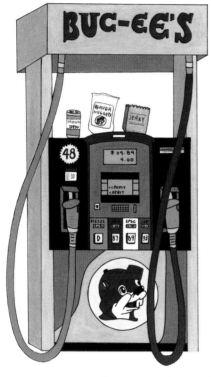

tended to mean little more than a Coca-Cola.

The convenience mart came about in 1927 when the Southland Ice Company in Dallas, Texas, set out to capitalize on the limited hours of grocery stores. They sold staples—bread, milk, and eggs—from their ice docks later than the norm. And, by 1946, they had expanded their stock, locations, and hours to become 7-Eleven, open 7 a.m. to 11 p.m., seven days a week. By the '60s, convenience stores had seamlessly united with gas stations, capitalizing on drivers' needs and whims. For its part, 7-Eleven introduced the Big Gulp (thirty-two ounces of soda) in 1976, followed by the Double Gulp (sixty-four ounces) in 1988. All of the giant Gulps were later tapered in order to fit into average cup holders.

It's reported that about 25 percent of Americans now live within a mile of a 7-Eleven store, though that's less often the case in the South. Of the company's more than nine thousand locations, six southern states claim zero (and Kentucky counts just one). Still, for many rural outposts, the kind of convenience mart that 7-Eleven spawned provides the closet marketplace for food. Within the 765 square miles of Holmes County, Mississippi, there were reportedly just four groceries in 2017, outnumbered three to one by corner stores and gas stations. So residents, including many without cars, are left to embark on long drives to find ingredients for meals.

Between trips, "gas stations pinch hit," writes documentarian Kate Medley. "And contrary to popular narratives, that doesn't always equate to Hot Cheetos and Mountain Dew." Like the fried chicken at Sanders's café in Corbin, Kentucky, many service stations prepare dishes that reflect their region or owner. In Avon, Mississippi, Maddox Grocery stuffs boudin sausage. About thirty-five miles northeast in Indianaola, Betty's Place plates buffalo fish ribs. In Raleigh, North Carolina, La Cabana Taquería, tucked in the back of a BP, slings tacos with eggs and chicharrón. And in the county next door, a 76 in Calvander fries vegetable samosas. As co-owner Minesh Patel once put it, "Everybody needs food"—a place to fill up.

## FRATESI GROCERY and SERVICE STATION
### LELAND, MISSISSIPPI

I top off my tank at Fratesi Grocery and Service Station. But the sign fastened to a wooden box of minnows out front says the place is something more: "EAST-LELAND-MALL & COUNTRY CLUB." My hunch is confirmed by the deli case inside, which is stocked with Genoa salami, mortadella, ham, and Italian sausages. Then there's the menu, displayed between two mounted bucks and featuring po' boys, muffalettas, and from-scratch gumbo and spaghetti sauce.

"It's hard to compete with other convenience stores gas-wise," says Mark Fratesi, who co-owns the shop with his two brothers. "We evolved into more of a deli to stay in the game." That's putting it mildly. To label Fratesi's a simple gas station or deli is akin to calling a Rolls Royce any old car. Housed in what looks like a standard convenient mart off Highway 82 in the Mississippi Delta, Fratesi's has the expected chips, ice-cold sodas, and beers. But it also sells bait, deer mounting hangers, and those fine meats and sandwiches.

Brothers Tony and Larry Fratesi, the children of Italian immigrants, opened the original service station in 1941—a simple wood-framed building not far from the current location that sold gasoline and a smaller selection of cigarettes, beer, and groceries. As they did then, the Fratesis

still farm, tending soybeans, corn, and cotton, and they cater to other local farmers. Honoring the tradition that Tony Fratesi began decades ago, they also still let folks gather after a long day in the fields for a happy hour that starts at around 5:00 p.m. Beers are tallied in a ledger to pay for later, with hand-scrawled names forming something of a register for the East Leland Country Club.

When I roll in a little after 10:00 on a Saturday morning, the store is quiet: a couple of folks buying gas, a few others, biscuits. I order a muffaletta—a pile of Italian charcuterie and chopped olive salad that's served on sesame bread. Fratesi's muffalettas rival those of New Orleans, where the sandwich supposedly originated at Central Grocery in 1906, but that makes sense. Many of the Delta's Italian residents immigrated through or first lived in Louisiana, bringing with them a taste for Italian, Creole, and southern food traditions.

I wait until I'm a few hours down the highway to eat my sandwich, until the olive salad has had time to seep into the bread and to unite the different ingredients. It's not unlike Fratesi's, where disparate goods—pecans, hay, diesel, deli sandwiches—come together under a green metal roof, one that reflects the Delta all around it.

# HYPERBOLE

Over the course of thirty days in Europe, seventeen people approached Katie Hurley, recognizing her Dinglewood Pharmacy T-shirt from Columbus, Georgia, and its "Almost Famous" slogan. "She kept a log of those people," says Terry Hurley, Katie's father and Dinglewood's owner. "So we are 'Almost Famous.'" The claim is an understatement for the Dinglewood, which, being more than a century old, has more than made its mark on the world with offerings like the Scrambled Dog—a chopped up hot dog and bun that's served in something like a banana split boat, smothered in chili and topped with oyster crackers and pickles. It's also a modest tagline for a hot dog, surely one of the most boasted-about foods around.

The tone for frank braggadocio dates back to 1916, when Nathan Handwerker opened a stand on Coney Island. He sold his hot dogs for a nickel, half the price of those of his nearest competitor, and by 1925 declared them "Nathan's Famous." "And what chutzpah . . . to call his fledgling company 'famous,'" his grandson William wrote, decades later. "Yes, the business was growing steadily and gaining popularity, but it was far from the household word or 'phenom' it was destined to become. And it surely was not even close to being famous in 1920."

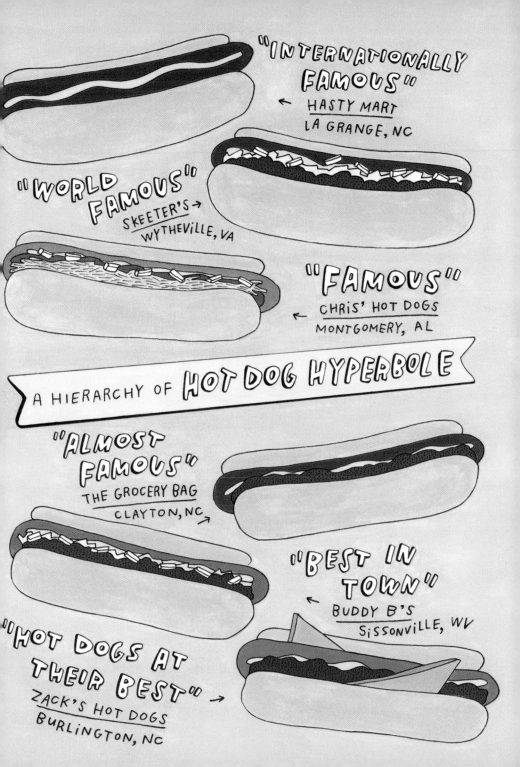

"INTERNATIONALLY FAMOUS"
← HASTY MART
LA GRANGE, NC

"WORLD FAMOUS"
SKEETER'S →
WYTHEVILLE, VA

"FAMOUS"
CHRIS' HOT DOGS ←
MONTGOMERY, AL

A HIERARCHY OF HOT DOG HYPERBOLE

"ALMOST FAMOUS"
THE GROCERY BAG
CLAYTON, NC →

"BEST IN TOWN"
← BUDDY B'S
SISSONVILLE, WV

"HOT DOGS AT THEIR BEST" →
ZACK'S HOT DOGS
BURLINGTON, NC

ALMOST FAMOUS
# THE ^SCRAMBLED DOG

Hyperbole is a half-truth, part veracity and part audacity. Whether a place is self-proclaimed "best," "famous," or "amazing," the label conveys a confidence that says it's worth its stuff. As Bud Sanderson of Sandy's Famous Hot Dogs in Columbia, South Carolina, admits, "We said we were famous the day we opened up." All that matters to Sanderson is that he backs it up. "We've always been 'famous,'" he repeats, "but we're recognized in the market." Dave Paul, the third-generation owner of Paul's Place Famous Hot Dogs in Rocky Point, North Carolina, also emphasizes supporting the claim, saying his dad "sold a million [hot dogs] before he called it famous." He's quick to add, "We've sold over 100 million now."

Hand-painted lettering on the side of Skeeter's World Famous Hot Dogs in Wytheville, Virginia, which opened in 1925, announces "9 million sold," a previous "6" slashed through. But Wanda Rodgers, the manager, has no idea about today's count. She's also not sure about the origin of "World Famous," though she believes it. "We have people from all over the world coming in," she says. Terry Hurley believes there's a worldliness to the Dinglewood, too. "We've had a great deal of notoriety," he says. "We've catered weddings in Saudi Arabia and Florence. We fed Prince Charles when he was at the 1976 Bicentennial in Atlanta." Perhaps that's why the Dinglewood's Styrofoam cups now say "World Famous" in a blue script. "Famous means different things to different people," says Hurley. On the road, you can bet it means delicious.

# CROMER'S P-NUTS

COLUMBIA, SOUTH CAROLINA

"Many nuts . . . pass through these doors." I accept the invitation stenciled in yellow on the entrance to Cromer's P-Nuts and step inside to learn about the biggest nut, Julian D. Cromer. Around 1937, the peanut patriarch from Lexington County, South Carolina, labeled his roast the "Guaranteed Worst in Town," responding to a neighboring vendor at the Columbia Farmers Market who declared his the very best and wouldn't shut up about it. The saying stuck.

"'Worst in town' precedes this place," says Rob Turner, Cromer's great-grandson. "People on the road know it's hotter than heck here and it's got the guaranteed worst peanuts." In case it's not clear, a hand-painted triptych underscores the point. "If you find a good p-nut in your pack / return it," one panel announces. "Our mistake."

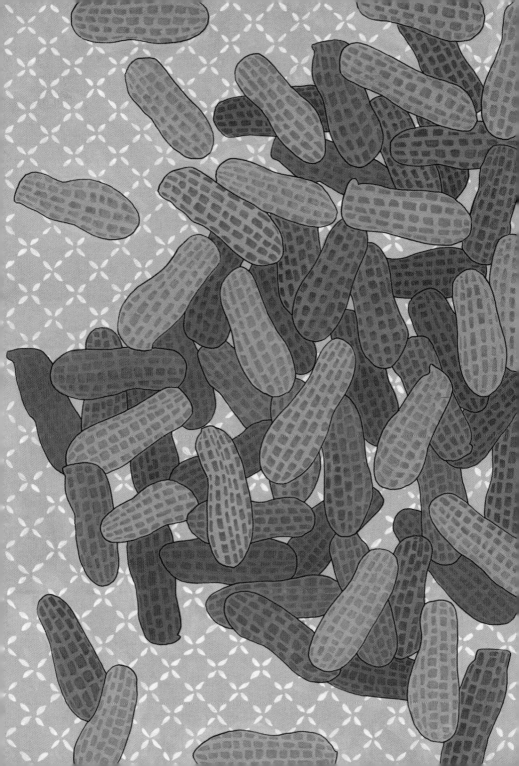

Cromer's knows its audience. Having expanded in the 1950s to offer all manner of concession and vending supplies—from gumball machines to popcorn kernels and snow-cone syrups—there's an emphasis on fun and wit. For decades, Cromer's sold costumes and makeup. And in the 1970s, it housed seven capuchin monkeys at a satellite location in Dutch Square mall, seemingly just for the hell of it. "One got out and ran all over the mall," Carolette Cromer Turner recalls. Today, the only monkeys are plush toys stocked between burlap bags of peanuts, and the mall location has shuttered.

Cromer's has seen its share of storefronts. A faulty popcorn machine sparked a fire at its second home on Assembly Street in 1993, causing it to shift locations. And since 2000 alone, the business has switched spots three times, finally landing at its current home on Main Street, where a new bay of windows lets customers see popcorn as it's popped and cotton candy as it's spun. But by and large Cromer's has stayed the same family business. "We've all worked here at some point," says Carolette, Julian's granddaughter, who took over in 2006, and whose sons Rob and Christopher also hold positions in the company. In eighty-some years only three men have boiled Cromer's peanuts, and they've all been related. But most importantly, the nuts are still the worst—at least in name. "Guaranteed not enough / p-nuts in a pack / to make you sick," a sign reassures. Convinced, I hit the road with a bag of boiled peanuts.

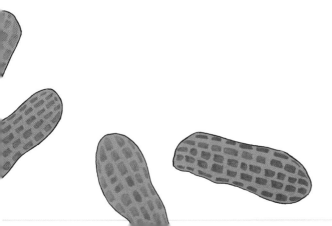

# ICONS

Before he put on a white suit and thin black bolo tie to become the Colonel, Harland Sanders squeezed into a stack of white tires, dressing the part of Bibendum, Michelin's rubbery mascot. The gig didn't last long. It was just another dead-end job on a long list, which also included railroad worker and legal assistant. But in the early 1920s, it signaled what was ahead for Sanders—a career built along the burgeoning highway, and an immortal role as the face of Kentucky's "finger-lickin' good" fried chicken.

On the road, that face meant a lot. Icons— from a golden arch to a white castle, a pigtailed girl to a goateed colonel—can offer consistency in unknown territory. They are symbols to fall back on or to glean for information, often representative of both product and a place. For the peanut belt of Virginia, and later for peanuts everywhere, the symbol was the ever-trim Mr. Peanut.

1990s CARTOON COLONEL

First sketched as "a little peanut person" by fourteen-year-old Antonio Gentile of Suffolk, Virginia, who won five bucks for a contest entry in 1916, Planters's Mr. Peanut rose from the dusty fields of Southside, Virginia, to the pinnacle of Times Square,

displayed in 6,700 lights over 47th Street. With his mono-
cle, top hat, and cane, he lent status to the lowly legume,
touting its prowess as a health nut packed with protein in
advertisements everywhere, from the *Saturday Evening
Post* to subway cars bound for Coney Island. But as folklorist Rachel Kirby notes, "De-accessorized, Mr. Peanut
is just a creature of the earth." He's the planter and the
planted, both a member of the Virginia aristocracy and
a product of its fields.

1950s
MR. PEANUT

Harland Sanders had his Oxfords in two worlds,
too. The founder of Kentucky Fried Chicken built his
brand on a dish that was the hallmark of Sunday
suppers and humble southern cooking. And he did
so as the Colonel, a meaningless designation bestowed by
the governor of Kentucky that seemingly linked him to the
Confederacy and afforded an air of Old South authenticity.
White tourists ate it up, charmed by his then black suit and
bleached white beard, and by his second wife, Claudia, who was known
to dress in antebellum regalia and parade around the dining room of the
Sanders Café and Service Station in Corbin, Kentucky—an early iteration
of KFC.

But Sanders was also moving forward—and in a white Cadillac, no less.
In the Caddy, packed with sacks of seasoned flour and a pressure cooker
he called Bertha, he took his business on the road, offering mom-and-pop
restaurants as far away as Utah the opportunity to place official Kentucky
Fried Chicken on their menus. In lieu of a customary skillet, Sanders used
a pressure cooker to quickly fry drumsticks, breasts, and wings, inspiring
a flock of chicken chains to follow, including two supported by singers,
Minnie Pearl's Fried Chicken and Mahalia Jackson's, as well as North
Carolina's Bojangles and Louisiana's Popeye's.

The Colonel's goateed face sold—so much so that when Jack Massey and John Y. Brown Jr. bought the company in the 1960s, they also purchased the rights to Sanders's image, keeping him on as something of a living icon for an initial salary of $40,000 a year. "He wasn't just a trademark. He wasn't somebody that an adman had made up, like Aunt Jemima, Colonel Morton, or Betty Crocker," Brown once said. "He was a real live human being and a colorful, attractive, persuasive one."

Sanders was an outspoken one, too. In the years after he sold Kentucky Fried Chicken, his opinion of the company diminished. Visiting a Manhattan-based Kentucky Fried Chicken with Mimi Sheraton of the *New York Times*, the Colonel declared its offerings "the worst fried chicken I've ever seen." With his fiery mouth (Sanders once planned a trip to Australia to supposedly remedy his cussing), he was an icon on the lam. It's no surprise, then, that after he died in 1980, KFC eventually replaced him in commercials with a jovial (and controllable) cartoon. That Colonel laughed and danced and tapped his cane. Next, a slew of celebrities, including Rob Lowe, were hired to portray the legendary founder in television commercials. Clad in a white astronaut's uniform, a thin black bolo tie painted on its front, he vowed to take crispy chicken "to new heights."

## HARLAND SANDERS CAFÉ AND MUSEUM
### CORBIN, KENTUCKY

Brass railings surround the kitchen of the original Sanders Café, cordoning off the Colonel's Vulcan range and Hobart mixer, his neatly stacked dishes and a row of rusty spice cans. Seated at tables in a dark, wood-paneled dining room, restored to its 1940s prime with Harland Sanders's name etched in glass windows that look out on Highway 25—the old Dixie Highway—folks dine on the Colonel's eleven-spice chicken. Thighs and drumsticks are fried in an adjoining fluorescent light–filled room, a

# THE SPORK

ALMOST
AS
ICONIC
AS
THE
COLONEL

modern-day KFC that doubles as part of the Harland Sanders Café and Museum.

The space opened in 1990 on what would have been the Colonel's one hundredth birthday. For the occasion, JRN, a company that runs some two hundred KFC franchises (including the one at the café), made an appeal for Colonel memorabilia. The result, displayed in a wall of glass cases, includes Sanders's white suit, a pressure cooker and two butcher knives, and an original menu featuring a Kentucky Ham Breakfast for $1.70, advertised as "Not Worth it—But Mighty Good." The Colonel's image also shows up throughout—as a bronze bust, the crux of a weather vane, the face of a nine-foot-tall highway sign, a bobble head, and a glossy white statue that sits cross-legged on a bench. A highway marker in front of the building describes him as "Kentucky's Most Famous Citizen."

Almost as prevalent as the image of Harland Sanders is that of his fried chicken. And, beyond imagery, its aroma fills the restaurant and museum, eventually tempting visitors like myself away from the display cases and interpretive panels and toward the restaurant's counter. There, I order a Fill Up box special—a drumstick and thigh, a biscuit, a side of mashed potatoes with gravy, a cookie, and a glass of tea. At the last minute, I also add a KFC button, which proclaims, "I ate where it all began!"

# J

## JUNQUE

"Get out of the water. Get out of the water. A shark attack is about to occur!" With this capstone cry a Shark Attack cocktail is served at a neon-lit Tropical Isle bar on Bourbon Street. The drink hinges upon cheap trinkets and a performative pour: a bartender places a small toy alligator into a cup of blue-syruped vodka, then dunks a plastic shark—its jaw brimming with red grenadine— into a cocktail while ringing a bell, blowing a whistle, tossing a stack of napkins into the air, and shouting. Slightly lesser known than Bourbon Street's beaded necklaces, the Shark Attack's shark similarly serves as a memento of a raucous time—or, in some cases, a reminder of something only dimly remembered. As author Brett Martin has written of a brush with the cocktail, "The next morning, feeling less than 100 percent, I put on my coat, felt something strange in the pocket, and opened it to find a plastic shark, its insides still sticky with grenadine residue."

Historian Ted Ownby posits that souvenirs reveal what a person deems "extraordinary" about an experience. They are hauled home from destinations and displayed to signify or commemorate (to others, or to oneself) an uncommon occurrence. But more than sparking a memory, souvenirs like the plastic shark can also anticipate an experience. Tourists descend on Bourbon Street expecting a drunken night, and the shark—which would otherwise be considered a child's toy—fulfills the promise with its boozy grin. Basically, place begets product, product evokes place. Across Florida, for instance, tourists have expected tropical wares since at least the 1880s. Then, Jacksonville's Bay Street was fondly called "Curio Row" for its stock of palmetto and seashell tchotchkes, and Main Street went by the name "Alligator Avenue," a nod to the sharp-toothed trinkets peddled there.

Beyond place, objects also say something about their makers—or at least their makers' perceptions and beliefs. Charles Reagan Wilson, former director of the Center for the Study of Southern Culture, traces mass-produced tchotchkes back to the late nineteenth century, when fans of the Confederacy (or those wishing to capitalize on it) placed images of Robert E. Lee and Stonewall Jackson on all manner of things, including knives, cards, and bottles of whiskey. Interestingly, many of the creators of those products were not from the South, which remained a place of agricultural production. Instead, northern companies created goods that they imagined southerners would favor.

Wilson, who owns one of the largest collections of southern kitsch—what he calls his

A SNAPPY SOUVENIR

FLORIDA

Southern Tacky Collection—became enamored of mass-produced stuff as a child, when his family moved from one corner of the South to another, then made road trips in between. "What possibilities those 3,000 miles from West Texas to Tennessee held!" he once mused. "Frontier-village amusement parks, tourist meccas like Six Flags Over Texas, animal farms with snakes and alligators—each had a souvenir to buy and save. And, oh, how many times did we stop at Stuckey's?"

According to Bill Stuckey Jr., the teal-roofed gas stations were strategically positioned along highways where travelers returning from vacations in Florida and surrounding states could easily access them. "People whose trips were nearly over were better prospects for buying unnecessary things like seashell lamps and rubber alligators," writes Tim Hollis, another southern knickknack scholar and collector. Similarly, to capture tourists no matter the direction they were traveling in, Alan Schafer built Mexico Shop East and Mexico Shop West on either side of the highway at South of the Border, his sprawling roadside attraction in Hamer, South Carolina. The stores overflow with bins of stuff that represent some misplaced notion of Mexico, including sombrero-shaped ashtrays and "Pedro" figurines. "Fill Yo' Trunque Weeth Pedro's Junque," a billboard proposes to cars on I-95.

## PARKWAY BAKERY AND TAVERN
### NEW ORLEANS, LOUISIANA

Parkway's paper hats are still free, a sign of good times. "When it gets to the point we're selling the hats, we've either become a tourist trap or we aren't doing well," says the head chef and general manager, Justin Kennedy. It's midmorning on a Tuesday—Parkway's down day—and there's chuck roast in the oven, slow cooking for the lunch rush that will wind through the dining room and spill onto the patio on Wednesday.

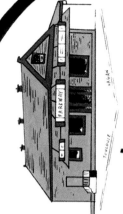

# Parkway EST 1911

## Home of the New Orleans Poor Boy!

PAPER HAT ←

POOR BOY → BEADS

TINY NOTEBOOK WITH ↙ TINIER PEN

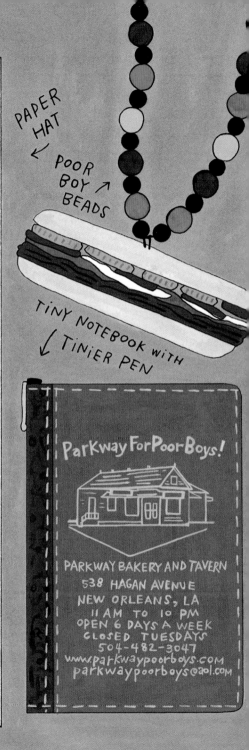

Parkway For Poor Boys!

PARKWAY BAKERY AND TAVERN
538 HAGAN AVENUE
NEW ORLEANS, LA
11 AM TO 10 PM
OPEN 6 DAYS A WEEK
CLOSED TUESDAYS
504-482-3047
www.parkwaypoorboys.com
parkwaypoorboys@aol.com

The New Orleans poor boy shop (the restaurant prefers the full spelling to po' boy) is less a tourist trap than a destination and neighborhood anchor. "We've met presidents and all sorts of celebrities," says Kennedy. (Obama had a shrimp poor boy when he visited during the fifth anniversary of Katrina.) "But the people that are important to me are the everyday people," he says.

Parkway Bakery and Tavern was founded by Charles Goering Sr. in 1911, a time when almost every New Orleans neighborhood claimed a corner bakery. In 1922, Henry Timothy Sr. bought the business, offering fresh breads and donuts. But Parkway's current era took root around 1929, when Bennie and Clovis Martin, former streetcar conductors who owned Martin Brothers restaurant, popularized (some say created) the po' boy sandwich, which they handed out to "poor boys"—Division 194 of the Amalgamated Association of Electric Street Railway Employees, who were on strike.

Across town, other bakeries, including Parkway, began offering the poor boy, a sandwich whose signature is its New Orleans–style French bread with a soft interior and thin outer crust. According to Parkway company history, they handed out sandwiches stuffed with French fries for free, and also sold them to workers at the American Can Company and Higgins Industries, also located in Mid-City. Parkway struggled after the American Can Company closed in 1988, and in 1993, the Timothy family sold the business. Not long after, Kennedy's uncle Jay Nix, who lived next door on Hagan Avenue, purchased the building and used it to house materials for his construction business. "He'd go all over the city and brag that Parkway was his storage shed," says Kennedy. "You'd hear all these stories."

At the behest of old customers, Nix eventually gave in, reopening Parkway in 2003 with the help of Kennedy, who was then a college student. "I thought this was just a pass-through," he says of joining the

# THE POOR BOY*

☆ A THING OF IMPERMANENCE

business. But after Katrina flooded the building in 2005, Kennedy came on full-time, helping resurrect Parkway once again. Inside, the walls serve as something of a New Orleans scrapbook, with a photo of Hubig's Pies, a menu from Brennan's, a pennant from the Saints, and so on. "Ninety percent of this stuff was given to us by customers," says Kennedy. For its own mementos, Parkway doles out the free folded caps. It also sells baseball hats, T-shirts, koozies, Mardi Gras beads (with a poor boy dangling at the bottom), and tiny leather notebooks that are embossed with an image of the Parkway building and come complete with tiny pens.

"Most of the stuff we sell is edible. It's gone and we like to give people something to take home," says Kennedy. "[The hats] remind people we're around. This place will be here when we're dead and gone."

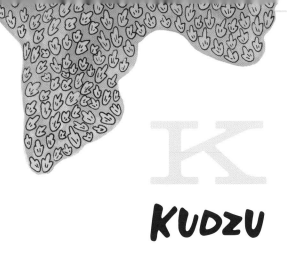

# K

# KUDZU

Edith Edwards slowly backs a minivan out of a carport, KUDZU spelled out across her North Carolina vanity plate. "It was a mistake to plant it," she says of the spindly bamboo shoots that surround the building. "It's invasive." Then Edwards cuts across the nearly four-hundred-acre farm that's been in her husband's family for more than two centuries and heads toward Mary's Meadow.

There, kudzu curls up and over the banks of Clarence Henson Road before crawling forty acres across Kudzu Cow Farm and clambering up the trees. It's a scene that would have enthused Channing Cope and the twenty thousand members of his Kudzu Club in the early 1940s. Then, the expanding highway system had left shoulders like that of Clarence Henson Road unstable, with shifting sand and topsoil that had been depleted by the long-nosed boll weevil, the loathsome bug that killed King Cotton. "And this brings us to the miracle plant *kudzu*," Cope wrote in his man-ifesto, *Front Porch Farmer*, in 1949. "There is nothing like it for the holding and building of those red barren hills."

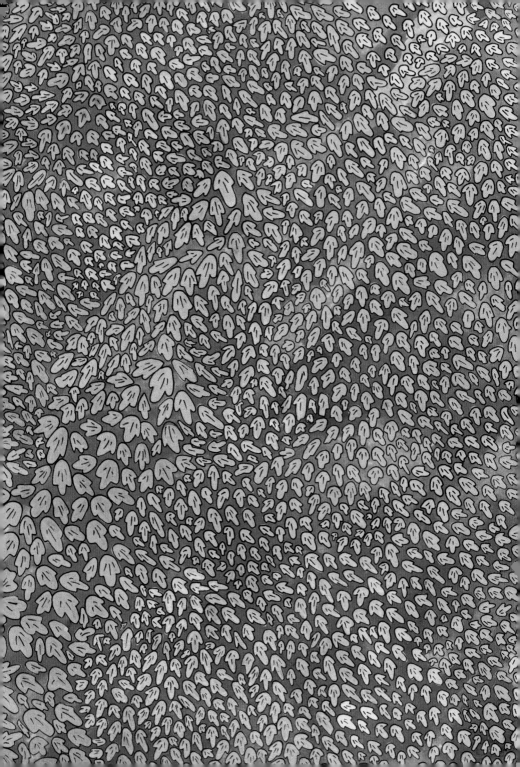

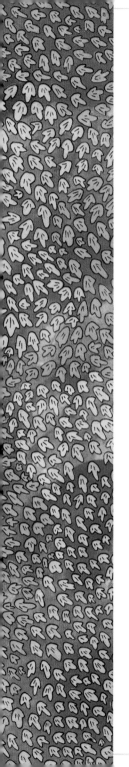

Over the sixty-year period after the vine was first introduced to the United States by Japan at the Centennial International Exposition of 1876 in Philadelphia, the first official World's Fair in the United States, kudzu had its share of promoters. Most notably, the Soil Conservation Service (which developed out of the Soil Erosion Service) touted its promise, harvesting seventy million seedlings to plant and paying anyone who would do so up to eight dollars an acre. Knitting together shaky soil, feeding livestock, and depositing much-needed nitrogen as it grew, the vine gave as promised. But it also took, growing strands that could multiply up to a foot a day and stretch to one hundred feet in length. "For some reason, possibly the fact that the miracle vine will run up on trees and telephone wires and will take over yards and empty lots in city areas, there has arisen a great prejudice against kudzu," Cope wrote in 1949.

As the vine scrambled its way across the region, its enthusiasts dwindled. And by the 1970s, the Department of Agriculture considered it a nuisance. Kudzu even claims space under the Federal Noxious Weed Act, which aims to control and eradicate pernicious plants. But none of that deterred Edith and Henry Edwards, who, in their nineties, have been growing kudzu for more than seventy-five years. This set the Edwardses apart from almost all other people; these days the supposed

"vine that ate the South" is more often chopped and hacked, burned and sprayed. But with the help of their son Duncan, a retired geologist, the Edwards cultivate it, baling kudzu like hay to feed livestock. "Any animal who eats forage will love kudzu," Henry once said, from his recliner. In the '60s, he fattened his dairy cows on the vine.

At the Edwards homestead, however, kudzu isn't just for goats and cattle. "I tried my first kudzu leaf on August 22, 1981," Edith says. "Red letter days. You never forget." Edith was inspired to eat the leaf after receiving a copy of *The Book of Kudzu* from a relative. Published in 1977, it contains more than seventy recipes and advice for medicinal uses. Edith began with a lightly battered leaf that she quickly fried. "I had to laugh," she says, still giddy more than thirty years later. "Henry said, 'What in the world is happening in the kitchen?' And I said, 'You won't believe it.'"

Edith steeps leaves for tea and turns purple kudzu buds into jelly. "Fresh blossoms taste like grapes," she says. "Frozen blossoms taste like apples." She's wearing a green kudzu-dyed T-shirt and a hat that she fashioned from a dried vine. Actually, she admits, the hat was initially conceived of as a basket, but a reporter once asked her to wear it for a photo before dubbing her the Kudzu Queen. "I sort of forgot about that title," she says, looking over a scrapbook. "But I'm ninety now and it's not so bad having a title."

# COATES PRODUCE

## ASHEVILLE, NORTH CAROLINA

HOW TO
CONTAIN KUDZU

**COATES PRODUCE**

**Kudzu Blossom Jelly**
Ingredients: Kudzu Blossom Juice, Pure
Cane Sugar, Pectin, Citric Acid

Net Wt: 10 oz (283g)
Made locally for Coates Produce
WNC Farmers Market
Asheville, NC

Shelved near the common fig preserves and orange marmalade, Coates Produce keeps jars of honey-toned kudzu jelly. "The worst thing about the kudzu," says Michael Coates, "is it's so dang invasive. It's good that there are some uses for it." That was news to Coates, a farmer in Madison County, North Carolina, where the vine creeps up and spills out across shady hills and trees. "We had kudzu and it was more of a nuisance than anything else," he says of his childhood on the farm. Now he also sees it as a light spread for biscuits, though he doesn't eat it often.

The same is true for Robin Pridmore, who makes the jelly (and about 149 other varieties of preserves) for private labels like Coates's. "Mama started it," she says. "There ain't no telling where she heard about it." Pridmore's inflection hints that she finds the popular jelly amusing, so I ask how she would describe it to the uninitiated. "You don't want to know," she laughs. "It's got its own flavor. It all depends on the person's taste."

When I purchase a jar from Coates at the Western North Carolina Farmers Market, he says it reminds him a little of a plum, then places the jar in a brown paper sack for me to carry with me. "I think [people] buy it because of the novelty," he tells me later by phone. "Then they come back and buy more because they like it." On my way out of Asheville, I continually catch glimpses of kudzu clinging to the trees. Weeks later, the vine similarly hangs in my thoughts—and sticks to my toast.

# LANDMARKS

Democratic supporters in Evansville, Indiana, concocted a nutty, last-ditch effort to help Jimmy Carter secure the 1976 presidential bid. They built a grinning thirteen-foot-tall peanut sculpture out of fiberglass and chicken wire to resemble the peanut-farmer-turned-candidate, displayed it at a rally, then gifted it to Carter's hometown of Plains, Georgia, where it still resides as one of the most photographed landmarks in town.

Peanuts know a pedestal. In Ashburn, Georgia, the "World's Largest Peanut" long rested inside the rim of a giant crown, which was perched atop a fifteen-foot brick tower (the nut was toppled by Hurricane Michael in 2018, though there are plans to rebuild). And in Blakely, Georgia, a stone nut sits slumped on a traditional marker, "a tribute to the peanut, which is so largely responsible for our growth and prosperity." So proud is Dothan, Alabama, the self-proclaimed "Peanut Capital of the World," that the town erected multiple landmarks: a golden peanut; a cast of peanut people, which are supposed to represent famous folks from town; and a twenty-five-ish-foot-tall peanut, sporting the letters "USA," by the entrance to the National Peanut Festival grounds.

Landmarks do as their name suggests. They mark the land, designating a particular place as worth noting—though this is often subjective and as often debated. Who gets to build a monument reveals a person's

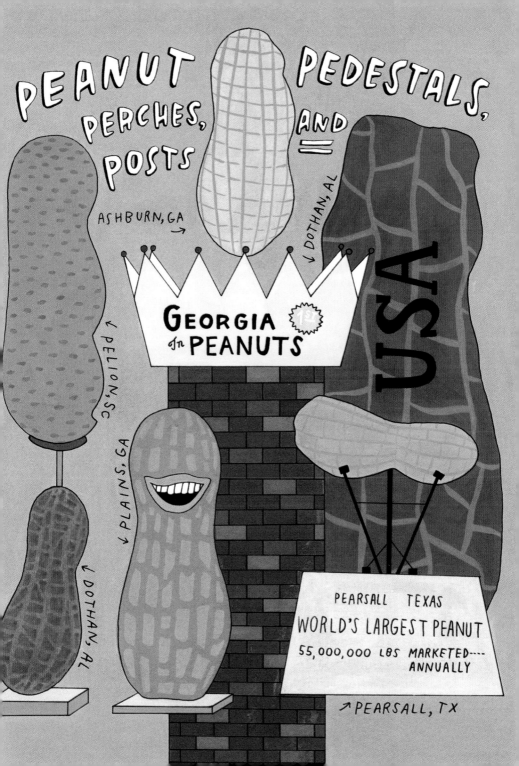

or a public's beliefs. (For instance, does it matter that George Washington Carver helped cultivate the peanut? Yes! The National Park Service concurs. Their monument to the esteemed botanist was their first to celebrate an African American person's contributions and to mark a non-president's birthplace. And does it matter that some Confederate general fought in a war? Sure, as it affected people's lives. But does it need a monument? No, thanks.)

## A PILLAR OF A PEACH

Other than giant rock outcroppings, such as Georgia's Lookout Mountain, agricultural pillars are some of the truest *land*-markings, elevating an entity of the soil—a concrete strawberry in Texas, an okra statue in Mississippi, a ceramic ear of corn symbolizing ancient Mexico. Almost as long as there's been agriculture, there have been sculptures to celebrate the bounty. As *Atlas Obscura* writes, "Sometimes there's only one way to prove how proud you are of something so small—build a monument to tell the world." In Gaffney, South Carolina, the Board of Public Works chair, Jack Millwood, proposed a peach-shaped water tower in 1975 to honor the stone fruit's local status. The result is the 135-foot Peachoid, which bares it all for drivers along I-85. With peach cheeks and a long crease, the tower has been the actual butt of many jokes. But it's also much beloved, the subject of dozens of photos each day. "If you have to be known for something, it might as well be a giant peach," Pam Wylie, an employee at City Hall, once told the *Los Angeles Times*.

GAFFNEY

In truth, Gaffney now produces few peaches compared to its previous output. So the Peachoid elevates an older story and provides some permanence. But landmarks aren't all about setting a piece of the past in stone (for one thing, stones crumble or can be knocked down). They can also help solidify hopes for the future. When Evansville's Democrats constructed their goofy peanut, their intent was serious. They sought to uplift a candidate who was grounded and weathered, a pillar of the community—much like the humble peanut.

## THE ORANGE SHOW

### HOUSTON, TEXAS

As we turn onto a quiet residential road in Houston, a citrus-themed castle comes into view with orange-colored enclaves, towers, spinning spires, and weathervane wheels. Dubbed the Orange Show, this shrine to the fruit is a three-thousand-square-foot landmark that artist Jeff McKissack began building out of found materials in 1956 and tinkered with until his death in 1980. "It's built like a fort. Extra Strong," he told *Texas Monthly* in 1977. "It's got to be. Weak construction would make the orange look weak as a nutrient. Strong construction makes it look strong."

But there are no actual oranges at the Orange Show, no cool juice to aid in waging war against Houston's noontime humidity. So my boyfriend, Land, and I wander heat-drunk through McKissack's tile and stone monument and start to believe it all. "TIME FOR ORANGES," one tiled wall announces. "GO ORANGE BE STRONG," says another. McKissack's proclamations are everywhere—spelled out on walls, visible from lookout posts, displayed in a little hut alongside a clown cutout and Santa's son, an unbearded mannequin in a red suit that McKissack scavenged from a cafeteria's holiday display. ("SANTA'S SON SAID 'I LOVE ORANGES. I'M

GOING TO MCALLEN, TEXAS AND PLANT A BIG ORANGE GROVE SO EVERYBODY CAN HAVE ORANGES FOR XMAS. DAD LOVE ORANGES. DAD KNOW BEST.'")

It's not clear when McKissack's obsession with the orange began, though there are clues. A 1930 census finds him as a young man in California, where he supposedly lived with a cousin just an hour from the National Orange Show, a monument to the California citrus industry. Following that, he reportedly spent time as a truck driver, hauling fruits in Florida and later Texas, where he also worked as a beautician and postman. By the late '60s, he was seemingly orange-obsessed. In addition to building his Texas landmark, McKissack penned a thirty-nine-page manifesto titled *How You Can Live 100 Years and Still Be Spry*, which emphasized the fruit's health benefits. McKissack died of a stroke two days shy of his seventy-eighth birthday.

According to his wishes, responsibility for the Orange Show fell into the hands of Marilyn Oshman, a Houston arts patron and friend who wanted it to become "a living, breathing monument." Now part of the Orange Show Center for Visionary Arts, it's weathered and rusted, but the whirligigs still spin and the monument more than impresses. It's a testament to McKissack's doggedness. "You could take a hundred thousand architects and a hundred thousand engineers and all of them put together couldn't conceive of a show like this," he once rightfully bragged. Nobody else could have created the Orange Show. It is completely McKissack. "LOVE ME ORANGE," he implores, a simple plea repeated on multiple signs throughout the monument.

# MEAT-AND-THREES

The way Dan Evins saw it, the high pressure under which Colonel Sanders was frying chicken had seeped into daily life. Southerners had traded high-backed chairs for stools or booths or car seats, swapping comfort for convenience. They'd dispensed with the dinner plate, eating out of disposable buckets or wax paper sleeves. And they'd rerouted, rushing around the South by way of the growing interstate. So Evins, often on the road as a rep for his family's oil company, dreamt of a place where travelers could sit down for a home-cooked meal. In 1969, he made one, founding Cracker Barrel by the side of I-40 where it cut through his hometown of Lebanon, Tennessee.

The original menu contained fast-food requisites—a "sho nuff" hamburger and a "skillet fried" hot dog. But it also featured homemade biscuits, a bowl of beans with onions and pickle relish, and greens flecked with hog jowl and finished with cornbread. These hot dishes resembled the hearty midday meals that southerners had long eaten to fuel days of hard work, a tradition they were reluctant to let go of. "As dinner for working people gradually moved from home kitchens to the cafes and restaurants of cities and towns," John Egerton wrote, "the pattern of heavy dining at noon was continued." Egerton chronicled the region's steam tables in his masterful *Southern Food: At Home, on the Road, in History*,

but he hardly needed to leave his base in Nashville to be convinced of their stature. "For reasons that are unclear," he claimed in the late '80s, "Tennessee is the leading Southern state in both the number and the quality of cafes, diners, and restaurants featuring traditional down-home cooking for lunch (and many of them also serve other meals)."

Still, Egerton, in his roaming, found many meat-and-threes—restaurants so named for plating one meat and three vegetables (macaroni among them)—shuttered or struggling. He suspected, as did Evins, that main streets, with their mom-and-pop restaurants and shops, were being swept away by the fast lanes that breezed past them.

Under these conditions, Cracker Barrel was in some ways an instant hit. Located immediately off an exit ramp and setting yesteryear's table in a building meant to look like an old country store, it met a real need. The first restaurants sold gasoline and turned rocking chairs into makeshift rest stops. And, as Egerton noted on his travels, in some places Cracker Barrel (and a smaller South Carolina competitor, Po' Folks) served the best, or even the only, hot "home-cooked" meal in town—a trend that continues. Today, there are more than 650 Cracker Barrels in forty-five

states. The menu includes references to real or imagined homes or people: Uncle Herschel's Favorite, a breakfast special, is named for Evins's actual relative; Momma's French Toast Breakfast reads as more vague. But the question nags, whose home does Cracker Barrel purport to be? And whom does it welcome?

Historian Angela Jill Cooley notes that, in 1969, on the heels of the civil rights movement, a restaurant meaning to replicate a country store "would have implied nostalgia for the racial etiquette that had permeated these spaces." At times in Cracker Barrel's history, such sentiments have been more blatant than a mere suggestion. In the early days, stores shelved Confederate memorabilia next to their old-fashioned candy. And in 2004, the Justice Department found about fifty locations guilty of discrimination against African American customers. These practices undermine the notion of the democratic dinner plate, which, at its best, brings all people together, whether on Main Street or off of I-40—beans and greens spilling over arbitrary dividers, and all the better for it.

## BULLY'S RESTAURANT

### JACKSON, MISSISSIPPI

It's about three miles from the I-55 exit to Bully's Restaurant, but after a few days on the road, we would drive at least a dozen more to eat a tray of fried chicken, black-eyed peas, macaroni and cheese, and the greens of the day. We're not alone. "I'll have them come in from Ridgeland and Richland and Pearl and Clinton," Tyrone Bully once said. "People are calling all the time to get the directions."

Bully's was conceived in 1982 as something of a short-order stop, but the restaurant shifted focus before its foundation was even finished. Out laying brickwork, Tyrone and his father, both trained masons, were approached by their neighbor Ma Pearl, who was in search of a job. She

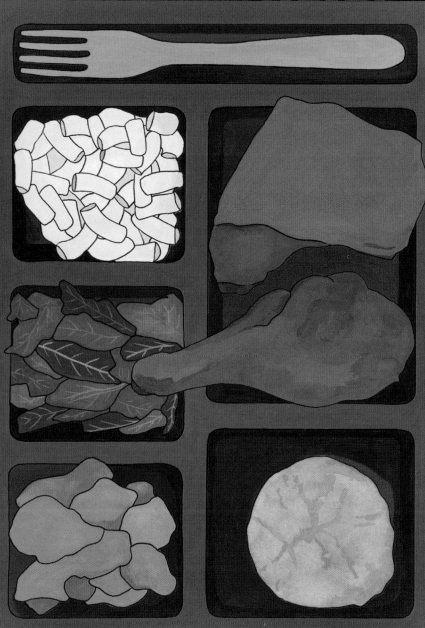

was known as a consummate cook, so they pretty much hired her on the spot, and learned from her in the kitchen for the next eighteen years. "She didn't mind telling you her secrets," Tyrone once told an interviewer. "She was the beginning and the backbone of this business, really." An early menu of burgers, pig ears, and smoked sausages fell out of favor once people tried Pearl's meatloaf, her beef tips with rice, and her smothered pork chops and greens—all of which Bully's still starts from scratch each day. As was the case on my initial visit to the meat-and-three, it's not uncommon to find a dining-room table piled with fresh greens, and a cook seated, stripping leaves from stalks.

In the restaurant's first days, customers included factory workers and neighbors from across the road. Then it was singers like Johnnie Taylor or the Williams Brothers, who recorded nearby at the legendary Malaco Records. And now it's just about everyone. Around the fiftieth anniversary of the civil rights movement, former Freedom Riders showed up to eat in Bully's small dining room, surrounded by portraits of Fannie Lou Hamer, Malcolm X, and President Obama. There are multiple images of Martin Luther King. "We set out to do a good job," Tyrone once said, "and we take it in the spirit of Dr. King when he said to do a good job and do that job so well that the living, dead, or the unborn couldn't do it any better."

It would seem that they do. In 2016, the James Beard Foundation designated Bully's as one of America's Classics. But even more telling, on a Monday in October, my red lunch tray is empty except for a few specks of greens and a smattering of cornbread crumbs. And yet we still order banana pudding.

# N
## NACKETS

Philip Lance got stuck with a raw deal—five hundred pounds of green peanuts—and roasted it, hawking the snacks for a nickel a bag in 1913. It was far from a novel move, as it mimicked enslaved Africans who had sold roasted peanuts on Market Street in Wilmington, North Carolina, before the Civil War, or Thomas Rowland of Norfolk, Virginia, who had shipped them to New York City, where they were distributed by Italian street peddlers, around the conflict's end. But it was smart, as legumes featured in a large swath of the nacket (cheap, light fare) industry in the South and well beyond.

Farmers like Tom Huston of Columbus, Georgia, who gleaned all that he could about peanut cultivation from George Washington Carver, began packing salted nuts in glassine sleeves before the Depression; under different ownership, Tom's brand of peanuts and sugary peanut bars later became vending machine staples. Starting in 1935, the Hardy family of Hawkinsville, Georgia, soaked peanuts in salt and dished them into briny bags to sell by the roadside (today they run more than twenty stands in central Georgia). And around 1915, Philip

Lance of Charlotte, North Carolina, ground nuts into butters that he and his family spread between cookies and crackers.

Chief among nackets is the notch-edged Nab. Nabisco coined the nickname in 1928, using it to market all manner of snack packs, including Oreos and Lorna Doones, and creating "NAB Diners"—primitive vending machines—to distribute them during the 1940s. But today, more often than not, the catchall term refers to a thin layer of peanut butter between two orange crackers. Lance called his version the Toastchee when he launched it in 1938. But the name's not necessary. No matter the brand, it's a Nab—the ruler of a road trip, the salve on a workday, the cornerstone of a country store.

Another darling of the corner mart is the combination of Coke and peanuts, a snack that writer John T. Edge believes "was likely born of country store commerce." "Think of Coke and peanuts as a prototype fast-food for the 20th century South," he has said. Advertised on metal signs affixed to buildings, Coca-Cola was one of the first widespread gas station offerings, and a handful of peanuts poured in added a punch of protein. It also made the snack convenient to consume while driving. "Any road trip was fueled by a sleeve of roasted and salted peanuts and a glass bottle of Coke," Edge, a native of central Georgia, has admitted.

Atkinson's little Peanut Butter Bar—a crisp candy wrapped in a handsome striped sleeve—lacked Coca-Cola's caffeine but still marketed itself as a "tasty energy food." Founded in 1932 by B. E. and Mabel Atkinson of Lufkin, Texas, the company focused on small cheap candies that Depression-era folks could afford (the Peanut Butter Bar debuted for just a penny). Not long after, Atkinson's introduced one of its most popular treats, the blazingly orange Chick-O-Stick—a confection made of peanut butter, sugar, and toasted coconut that rivaled sweets like Idaho's Chicken Bones and

STARS & STRIPES
FOREVER

was likely a nod to Sperry's Chicken Dinner candy made in Milwaukee. Priced at ten cents in the early '20s (and later slashed to five cents to reach a wider demographic), Sperry's popular chocolate-covered peanut bar was something of a precursor to the protein-packed Kind and CLIF bars that are so pervasive today. In name alone, Chicken Dinner put plainly how a small snack can keep a person going—between tasks on a factory floor, meetings at the office, or stops on the road. Or as Chick-O-Stick could claim, they contain a stick-to-itiveness.

# THE BEST STOP
## SCOTT, LOUISIANA

We had boudin and cracklins for breakfast, part of a complimentary Cajun platter at the Bayou Cabins near Breaux Bridge. We also had cracklins the night before, a paper sack full from Poche's Market that we crunched between swigs of beer on a porch that overlooked Bayou Teche. Still, when my boyfriend and I spot a sign for the Best Stop along I-10, we pull over for a snack. Among Cajun country's abundant purveyors of boudin and cracklins, the place proclaims itself as *the* best stop, and roadside hyperbole is a thing I tend to heed.

Stuffed boudin sausage and salty pork cracklins were once confined to backyard boucheries. "It was just . . . family and friends and . . . neighbors that would participate," Robert Cormier, Best Stop's cofounder, has said. But in the '80s, the outside world caught Cajun fever from TV celebrities like chef Paul Prudhomme and comedian Justin Wilson. Folks showed up in Acadiana

**BOUDIN. BOOYAH!**

← CRACKER

← CRACKLINS

looking for swamp tours, wild fiddling, and something to eat—boudin piled onto saltine crackers with a dash of Crystal hot sauce, an andouille-filled gumbo, or a spicy crawfish étouffée—and Cormier and his cousin Lawrence Menard realized they could feed them. The two had owned a small grocery in Lafayette, Louisiana, since the late '70s, and in 1986 they moved into a store off of I-10 to focus on local meats. They kept the former shop's name, The Best Stop, and their offerings live up to the hype, though Cormier would never admit that.

"We're not perfect," he demurs. But he also says, "We put our heart into everything we do. We take pride in our products." There are dozens—from andouille to tasso, crawfish tails, and alligator, and of course boudin and cracklins. The Best Stop sells between ten and fifteen thousand pounds of the sausage per week, along with sixteen hundred pounds of the crisp pork skins, maybe more during Louisiana's festival or football seasons—"anything that gets people traveling." Tourists don't always know what to expect. "They walk in and they seem kind of lost," Cormier says. "But I can't remember a time when I've given someone boudin and they didn't like it."

**ORIGINAL**

**"LOUISIANA"**

THE PERFECT

HOT SAUCE

ONE DROP DOES IT®

# OPEN

On an August afternoon in 2013, Buck Dickerson stood in the parking lot of his Durham, North Carolina, diner and wondered if he had a key to the front door. In the eight years he had owned Honey's, which opened under different management in 1960, he'd had little need for one, as the restaurant operated around the clock. But Dickerson managed to find it before 3:00 p.m., when he closed the door for good, the restaurant's lot having been leased to build a McDonald's.

THE NEVER-NEEDED KEY

NOPE! NEVER.

Access is central to the lore of twenty-four-hour diners. As scholar Katie Rawson writes, "A popular claim about Waffle House, which the company itself encourages, is that these always-open restaurants do not have locks." The comfort of buttery eggs and toast at any hour is clearly part of the appeal, but Lawson argues it's also about the "illusion of safety." "A place where people do not lock the doors does not just mean customers can come in anytime," she writes. "It also implies people are trusted."

The earliest twenty-four-hour diners hardly encouraged such feelings. Located in cities, they catered to industrial workers between shifts and were known for greasy food, salty language, and an unsavory atmosphere. Thomas Edison, who had a manufacturing factory on New York's Goerck

↓ ATLaNTa'S OTHER ALWAYS-OPEN CHaiN

Street, recalled "an all-night house" where he used to grab "lunch at two or three o'clock in the morning." "It was the toughest kind of restaurant ever seen," he wrote. "For the clam chowder they used the same four clams during the whole season, and the average number of flies per pie was seven. This was by actual count."

Edison eventually moved his plant out of the city to Schenectady, New York. By the late 1940s, many urban factories had also moved to the suburbs, where real estate was cheaper. To keep the lights on, twenty-four-hour hash houses had to try a different tack, becoming more family-friendly. This was a welcome shift in some regards. Following World War II, more families were eating out—in part due to busier schedules, since more women were in the workforce. So, many diners introduced children's menus and weekly dinner specials, hired women as wait staff, built family-sized booths, and installed jukeboxes—the latter appealing to teens looking for an after-school hangout. Part of the shift also involved a literal move from inner cities to blue-collar neighborhoods or lots by major thoroughfares, where elaborate neon signs beckoned drivers from the road.

The shiny diner of the 1950s served a diverse class of customers (though, racially, it veered more white until after the end of Jim Crow). As historian Andrew Hurley writes, "In addition to ladling goulash for hungry laborers and pouring coffee for tired truckers, countermen found themselves frying scrambled eggs for executives on their way to work, preparing sandwiches for female clerical workers on lunch breaks, and slicing pie for couples streaming out of nightclubs and movie theaters."

At twenty-four-hour restaurants, time is the great divider, carving out distinct dining windows for different groups. The crowd at midnight tends to be a little drunker, a lot blearier, and occasionally rowdier than the one at 9 a.m. But there's also a cozy around-the-clock sameness of wide booths, fried potatoes, and an open door.

# WAFFLE HOUSE MUSEUM

Pat Warner unlocks the door to the dullest Waffle House I've ever been in. There's no hash brown sizzle on the grill top, no "Hey, honey" from the wait staff, no Waffle House jukebox with its waffle-themed songs, and no customers—none drunk, none sober. Basically, it's nothing like Unit 1000 on the same street less than a mile away, where I just ate a plate of scattered, smothered, covered, and capped potatoes. Except that it is.

The Waffle House Museum, housed in the original Waffle House on College Avenue in Avondale Estates, Georgia, is a skeleton of the twenty-four-hour diners that dot interstates in twenty-five states. "You can trace a lot of stuff back to this first restaurant," says Warner, director of PR external affairs. The yolk-yellow booths are missing. But the setup of the counter, grill, waffle irons, and such are so much the same that Waffle House requires new managers to travel to Avondale Estates and spend time in the Museum as part of their training at Waffle House University. Listening stations play interviews with Tom Forkner and Joe Rogers Sr.— neighbors who founded the franchise a few blocks from their houses in 1955 (and who died just two months apart, both in their late nineties).

Joe Rogers Jr., who worked in the original location as a kid and now serves as chairman of the board, often leads the half-day trainings on site, speaking firsthand about his experience in the restaurant. In the exhibition room of the museum, a small space opposite the reconstructed dining room, a black-and-white snapshot shows Rogers Jr. behind the old Waffle House counter. Glass cases also display vintage uniforms, buttons, T-shirts, place settings, menus, and photographs, including one of members of the Avondale High School Class of '56, who used to walk down after school for waffles and coffee. A few years ago they held a reunion in this

# A HASHBROWN HOW-TO
## OR, LATE-NIGHT LINGUISTICS

SMOTHERED............SAUTÉED ONIONS
COVERED..............MELTED CHEESE
CHUNKED....GRILLED HICKORY SMOKED HAM
DICED................GRILLED TOMATOES
PEPPERED....SPICY JALAPEÑO PEPPERS
CAPPED....GRILLED BUTTON MUSHROOMS
TOPPED..............BERT'S CHILI™
COUNTRY........SAUSAGE GRAVY

side of the museum, one of many groups to do so. According to Warner, the space is particularly popular with bridal parties, which is oddly appropriate. Open all day and night, Waffle House has seen and served it all: the bleary and the wide-awake, the lone wolf and the troop, the local and the pilgrim, the sunny-side up, the cracked up, and the completely broken.

The all-day diner has a reputation for helping out in times of hardship. Informally, the Federal Emergency Management Agency is said to use a Waffle House Index to gauge a storm's severity, which basically breaks down to: it's not a good sign when the restaurant closes. During Hurricane Harvey in 2017, Waffle House sent in what it calls "jump teams"—management from other states—to fill in and cook a limited menu, keeping open most of Houston's thirty-six locations. "To be honest, we just cook bacon and eggs," Warner told NPR. "But sometimes you need bacon and eggs." Rephrased: in an hour of need, Waffle House is always there.

# PACKAGING

Laura Scudder made good use of her iron. In 1926, she steamed shut the opening of a wax paper bag to create the first airtight potato chip sack, and advertised her snacks as "the noisiest chips in the world." This claim was a feat made possible by packaging—an achievement that was later perfected by the Dixie Wax Paper Company of Dallas, Texas, which debuted preprinted, sealable bags. Earlier containers, like the hefty cracker barrels that were popular in nineteenth-century general stores or lidded five-gallon tins, were lousy at keeping a chip crisp or a cracker crunchy and were cumber-some to tote.

Absent colorful logos or slogans, most early packaging was also often mysterious. To borrow a lyric by Atlanta's Ludacris, "What in the world is in that bag? What you got in that bag?" The answer came in 1879 with the invention of the offset press, which branded every manner of bag and box. That same year, Robert Gair's paper-bag factory in Brooklyn, New York, made an accidental printing that resulted in foldable cartons. As reported in an issue of *Gair Today*, a printing press rule that was left too high

USE WITH STARCH *

* POTATO CHIPS

LAURA SCUDDER

NURSE, LAWYER, RESTAURANT OWNER,
RADIO & TV STAR, & CHIP BAG INVENTOR.

35¢

Laura Scudder's

potato
chips

THE
noisiest
chips
IN THE WORLD

net wt. 3 oz.

BASICALLY, ALL THAT AND a

BaG OF CHiPS.

"cut neat, but ruinous slits through several thousand paper seed bags before the mistake was discovered." Experimenting with press heights, Gair realized he could print a box from one sheet with indented seams to fold along.

Such boxes offered more than mere convenience. During the Jim Crow era, African American travelers, for whom unfamiliar restaurants and gas stations could mean violence or hostility, often packed shoeboxes stuffed with foods they could safely eat on the road—most notably, as scholar Psyche Williams-Forson has chronicled, fried chicken. So popular were drumsticks and wings on routes of migration that bones flung from car and bus windows paved a fabled "chicken bone express." Other staple foods included deviled or hard-boiled eggs, peanut butter and jelly sandwiches, biscuits, cheese, carrots, and slices of sweet potato pie or chocolate layer cake. As Williams-Forson posits, these shoeboxes allowed many southern African American women to travel physically, and for those who couldn't or didn't want to leave, to at least travel emotionally as their dishes made significant journeys.

Lunch cartons and containers also helped many women create jobs and find financial independence outside the home. In August 1917, Eugenia Duke spread pimento cheese and egg salad between slices of bread, packaging sandwiches in wax paper to take to a YMCA-run canteen at Camp Sevier near Greenville, South Carolina. With the help of her daughter, Martha, she sold them to soldiers for ten cents apiece, which covered the cost of the ingredients and the round-trip rail fare (about fifty cents) and turned a two-cent profit per sandwich. (It also gained her a loyal following, some of whom wrote letters requesting her famed mayonnaise—which she later bottled and sold simply as Duke's.) Company lore claims Duke sold ten thousand sandwiches in one day alone, making enough money to buy a delivery truck. Under a similar business model in Charlotte, North Carolina, Ruth Ross began packing tubs of mayonnaise-based salads and sandwich fillers in the 1950s, which she marketed as "Less Work for Mother." The spreads became staples of brown bag lunches eaten on road trips, factory floors, and school trays, and spawned their own fleet of delivery trucks (and around the 1960s, VW vans).

But for all the profits it generates, a container's convenience also clearly comes with costs. As the Dogwood Alliance, an environmental advocacy group headquartered in Asheville, North Carolina, has argued, fast-food restaurants' reliance on an array of paper packaging is destroying the southern woodlands, one of the largest paper- and pulp-producing regions in the world. In 2010, the group backed "Kentucky Fried Forest," a campaign whose mascot was a chainsaw-wielding Colonel Sanders, and who pressured the

EUGENIA DUKE

FOUNDER: DUKE SANDWICH CO., DUKE'S MAYONNAISE, & DUCHESS SANDWICH COMPANY

Duke's

HOME MADE QUALITY

MAYONNAISE

MADE WITH NATURAL INGREDIENTS FOR OVER 15 YEARS

Sugar-Free      NET 32 FL.OZS (1 QT)

PRETTY MUCH OUR

MOTHER MAYO.

Louisville-based KFC chain to shift toward more sustainable packaging options. Later that year, KFC (alongside Atlanta's Coca-Cola Company) snagged a Greener Package Award for its reusable polypropylene container for side dishes—what the company called its "best packaging idea . . . since the [chicken] bucket."

## SALLY BELL'S KITCHEN

### RICHMOND, VIRGINIA

Snow sprinkles the C. F. Sauer spice company's sign like salt from a shaker, but that isn't the main magic of this Monday—or any day—in Richmond. A few blocks down Broad Street, Sally Bell's Kitchen is deftly wrapping individual deviled eggs in wax Patty Paper without mashing them into a mess or ruining their fluffy yolks. And they've been doing so for almost one hundred years.

Sarah "Sallie" Cabell Jones founded Sarah Lee Kitchen (later named Sally Bell's Kitchen) in 1924 with Elizabeth Lee Milton, through the Richmond Exchange for Woman's Work, on the grounds of good food and good packaging. At a time when southerners increasingly found themselves away from home kitchens, portable lunches found favor on factory floors or in office break rooms, and in Sallie's opinion, any old paper sack wouldn't do. She set out to create

SALLY BELL'S KITCHEN
RICHMOND, VIRGINIA

BOXING CHAMP

the ideal thin white pasteboard box, working with Pohlig Bros., a local company that has manufactured the containers for decades. "It's probably one of the longest ongoing business relationships in all of Richmond," says Scott Jones, Sallie's great nephew. He orders around fifty thousand boxes each year—selling between 150 and 300 boxed lunches each day—all of which have to be folded. "When things slow down, we sit down and talk and fold boxes," Jones says. "My wife and I also take them home. She'll be watching the *Lawrence Welk Show* or *Seinfeld*, laughing and folding boxes, probably having a cocktail."

Part of the box's appeal is how snugly it holds the lunch combo: a sandwich, a side dish, a cheese wafer capped with a pecan, a cupcake turned upside down and iced around its edges (for maximum frosting), and one deviled egg half. To manage the threat of lunchbox intermingling, there's also some form of wrapping for almost all of the items therein (a paper cup for potato salad, plastic wrap for a ham sandwich, black-and-white deli paper to line the box, a ribbon to tie it up). It's a level of care inherent in the food, too. The eggs, for starters, are hard-boiled each morning, the yolks mixed with homemade mayonnaise and a hint of mustard, then sifted with paprika before being folded up in the paper sleeve. "It's a pain to wrap those things," says Jones, "You have to have a certain dexterity to do it. Not everyone can." Not everyone would either, but it's that attention to detail that has set Sally Bell's apart for nearly a century.

# QUE

In 1927, the *Rand McNally Auto Road Atlas* declared the road hog "the most obnoxious animal in the world." "He is as objectionable as any other hog and you can't eat him," the guide griped. But a drive through the South proves otherwise, as the whole region is whole hog. Smoked or salt-cured, basted or barbecued, stuffed into sausage or fat-fried into chicharrones, the southern pig is abundant and delicious—king of the roadside. It's no coincidence, then, that restaurant signs and billboards often depict hogs clad in crowns, top hats, or bowties.

But of all pork's cuts and preparations—of all southern foods, for that matter—it's barbecue that attracts some of the most fervent followers. They champion various styles of sauce (vinegar, tomato, and mustard-based, among them). They advance different spellings (barbecue,

↳ NAHUNTA PORK CENTER ~ PIKEVILLE, NC

↗ ABE'S BAR-B-Q
CLARKSDALE, MS

MR. BARBECUE↑
WINSTON~SALEM, NC

# PIGS OF PRESTIGE

OR, THE NOBLE BEASTS OF QUE COUNTRY

↙ LEONARD'S
PIT
BARBECUE
MEMPHIS,
TN

TOP HAT BARBECUE
↳ BLOUNT SPRINGS, AL

bar-b-que, BBQ, or simply q, que, or cue). They preach specific methods of slow cooking (wood-fired or gas, the most hotly debated). And they make known their preferences for pig parts (ham, shoulders, or ribs, if not the whole damn thing). They may even question the use of the hog. In Kentucky, barbecue is as likely to be mutton, and in Texas, it's commonly beef.

Southern barbecue's origins are often traced to the Caribbean where, in the early 1500s, Spanish explorers encountered folks using stick frames (structures called, or overheard as, *barbacòa*) to cook over open fires. Independently, Native North Americans also roasted meat on raised devices they called *barboka*. Such frameworks were later referred to as *barbecue*, and by the 1700s, that term was also employed to describe the food or the event at which it was served. Generally, they were large celebratory affairs, gathering entire families or whole communities. George Washington famously hosted and attended many barbecues, reporting in 1769, for instance, "Went in to Alexandria to a Barbecue and stayed all Night." But barbecues were, and are, as much for common people as for presidents. And therein lies que's appeal. Though divisive in theory, barbecue is at heart a great unifier, crossing lines of class and race. When it comes to barbecue on a plate, few folks will resist it.

Barbecues have historically been held in other locales, including up north. But by the late 1700s, they were most common in North Carolina and the Virginia Tidewater, where pigs were plentiful, having settled alongside colonists near Jamestown in 1607. Pigs were so populous by 1726 that William Byrd II of Westover, Virginia, described North Carolinians as a "porciverous" population whose "only business [was the] raising of hogs, which is managed with the least trouble, and affords the diet they are most fond of." Reacting to this claim, sociologist John Shelton Reed puts it another way. "With hogs cheap, plentiful, not hard to raise, self-basting, and easier than cattle to cook without dismembering, it's no wonder that pork became the preferred meat not just in North Carolina but across the South, right up to where East Texas gives way to cowboy country."

Other foods were barbecued in the Carolinas, including fish, beef, and chicken, but pork was preferred—the only meat claimed as *barbecue*. (Elsewhere, the term was sometimes employed to encompass an array of cheap eats, coinciding with the rise of the automobile. "Barbecue stands" just as commonly sold hot dogs or hamburgers to motorists.) Though barbecue is slow-cooked, it was in many ways well suited to the road. A whole hog affords a heap of meat that, once prepared, can quickly be piled onto sandwiches or plates. And so, by the mid-twentieth century, barbecue stands offering curbside service became popular fixtures in the South, attracting locals with a taste for que or travelers in search of something regionally "authentic."

Some folks tried their hands at franchising, including Jesse G. Kirby, who founded the Pig Stands Company in 1921. With Dr. Reuben Jackson as a partner, Kirby expanded, counting more than one hundred restaurants by the early '30s, as far afield as California. But, in general—at least compared to hamburgers or other quick-service offerings—barbecue has largely steered clear of the ubiquitous chain restaurant. In addition to the specialized skills required to slow-roast barbecue just right, tastes vary widely from place to place. As Reed writes, "Southern barbecue is the closest thing we have in the US to Europe's wines or cheeses; drive a hundred miles and the barbecue changes."

## CRAIG'S BAR-B-QUE
### DE VALLS BLUFF, ARKANSAS

Patterned with pheasants and ducks that rise and fall between snowdrifts, the peeling wallpaper at Craig's reminds me that I'm far from my temperate home turf in Eastern North Carolina. So does the menu, which finds

SUGGESTS WOOD-SMOKED PORK ↓

← DENOTES REMOTENESS

↓ GREASE (NOT GEESE) ↖

↗

# SAUCY SYMBOLISM
## OR, THE WRITING ON THE BARBECUE RESTAURANT WALLPAPER

← ALLUDES TO SLAW ON THE SIDE

IMPLIES WET-NAP NEEDED →
↓

beef and ribs alongside sliced pork. It's why I've made my way here to the Arkansas Delta. I'm curious what barbecue is like along this stretch of US Highway 70, an east–west route that cuts through my hometown and is something of a barbecue beltway in North Carolina, long studded with joints like Wilber's and Kings that preach chopped meat soused with peppery vinegar.

Craig's sits close to the two-lane road, less than a mile from downtown De Valls Bluff (a town name with varied spellings). Lawrence Craig established the restaurant in 1947 with his brother Leslie after working on a dredge boat on the Mississippi River. "Back when I was growing up there were two kinds of jobs black folks could get without being challenged by white folks," Craig once told writer John T. Edge. "Cooking and heavy lifting." On the water, chickens roamed the boat's roof and were later cooked along with beef and pork on an oil-flamed stove. Back in De Valls Bluff, Craig began barbecuing between voyages, then transformed it into full-time work. His signature creation was a thick, tart sauce developed with his wife, Alice—what their son Robert simply sums up as "originality." That's Arkansas barbecue, a thing that varies from place to place in the border state and is hard to tuck into one neat package.

The plate that arrives at my table contains a heap of pork, smoked over hickory in an open pit out back. Sauce swells up around the sliced meat, held in by Styrofoam dividers that also contain baked beans and frothy apple-specked slaw. To the side, there's a griddled bun and a small bag of Fritos, which are dropped off unannounced and unexplained. Nearly nine hundred miles across Highway 70, Craig's heavily sauced and thick-sliced barbecue is vastly different from the vinegary pulled pork I grew up eating in North Carolina. And yet, it's also the same—wholly revered.

# ROADS

Locke Craig, the fifty-third governor of North Carolina, put on a pair of overalls, picked up his tools, and went to work on a stretch of road in Buncombe County. "I call upon every able-bodied man to shoulder his shovel and march out and strike a blow for progress," he wrote in a 1913 proclamation that declared two mandatory Good Roads Days, during which North Carolina men were "to refrain from all other occupations" (for their part, women were encouraged to provide "faith and courage," as well as "good things to eat"). As the governor decreed, "It will be an honor to every man on these days to labor with his fellow-man to banish from the country the curse of bad roads and the evils that accompany them."

In 1912, North Carolina counted an estimated 48,000 miles of roads, with only 2,100 miles paved in gravel or macadam (tar-bound stone), and citizens like Craig became advocates of the Good Roads Movement—an initiative that was started in the late 1800s by touring cyclists mostly based in the North. In the South, where road building and maintenance were the responsibility of poorly funded counties, the movement initially targeted farmers, who depended on roads to transport crops.

Proponents across the region launched countless campaigns to spread the word—from Good Roads Days to exhibitions, driving tours and races, and lessons in road building. Still, progress was slow, as relatively few miles were built during mandatory workdays, and avid but inexperienced volunteers sometimes worsened existing roads through their efforts. Regardless, enthusiasm for roads grew as cars became more attainable for middle-class Americans. Roads promised freedom from the confines of a railroad timetable and provided folks a path out of places with prejudicial practices.

THE NORTH CAROLINA
GOOD ROADS ASSOCIATION
A State System of Hard
Surfaced Roads

An unabashed advocate of both the automobile and road expansion was Carl Graham Fisher, an Indiana native whose antics included fastening a Stoddard-Dayton to a hot-air balloon, then drifting in the car above onlookers in downtown Indianapolis. Fisher's mission was to convince the public that cars were safe, and he worked to try to make them so. His Prest-O-Lite company manufactured headlights, which helped cars maneuver easier at night and eventually turned Fisher and his partner James Allison into multimillionaires.

Fisher used his fortune to invest in the Indianapolis Motor Speedway, as well as a swath of land in Florida, which he first visited on his honeymoon. To aid travel to his new piece of real estate, Fisher proposed the "Cotton Belt Route," a north–south path that would connect several states (this was similar to his earlier idea for an east–west route, Lincoln Highway). Reconceived as the Dixie Highway, the course was also promoted as a way to grow businesses in small towns, as travelers would need places to stay, eat, and refuel. As such, everyone wanted in, resulting in a promotional arms race later named the "Second Battle of

Chattanooga" after the southern city where pivotal meetings were held. With no one able to agree on a single route, the result, begun in 1915, was two paths with points east and west. As historian Tammy Ingram emphasizes, "The idea that the route could accommodate multiple pathways at once transformed the Dixie Highway from a single long-distance road into an interstate highway network, the first of its kind in the United States and the most significant transportation development in the South since the region's first railroads."

Another important step occurred in 1916, when Congress passed the Federal Aid Road Act, which dispensed funds to state highway departments (this required that many southern states create such agencies). And in 1921, Congress passed the Federal Aid Highway Act, which named existing roads like the Dixie Highway as part of the Federal Aid Highway Road System, and provided fifty/fifty matching funds to build some of the nation's first major roadways. Progress sputtered along, as many states lacked dollars to make the matches, but the precedent was set for the federal government's investment in road building.

Southern roads were—and remain—fraught with obstacles. Their construction often cut off or completely ignored poor or rural communities, and they skirted downtowns, causing many businesses to shutter. Even so, the forging of new and better roads did, as North Carolina's Governor Craig hoped, "strike a blow for progress," unquestionably modernizing the region by connecting it to other areas.

## CRAWFISH SEAFOOD SHACK

### ATLANTA, GEORGIA

On a Sunday afternoon in August, I show up to a friend's house in Georgia looking suspect, dark spices lingering under my nails. "Where've you been?" she asks. The answer was Hieu Pham's Crawfish Shack, a restaurant that looks and feels like those customary along the back roads of Louisiana. Fishing nets hang from the ceiling and picnic tables are draped in checkered tablecloths, readied with paper towels and Louisiana hot sauce. But the Crawfish Shack is more than four hundred miles from the Louisiana Gulf Coast, situated in a landlocked strip mall off Atlanta's Buford Highway—a corridor legendary for its international cuisine.

Roads can be dividers, separating communities from one another, but they can also be powerful connectors, as in the case of Buford Highway. Stretching about thirty miles from Lenox Road to the city of Buford, the road brings together a myriad of ethnic communities, particularly along a six-or-so-mile stretch. Unlike concentrated neighborhoods found in other cities, such as New York's Chinatown or Little Italy, Buford assembles a multiplicity of backgrounds along a single sweep, a fact made visible on the restaurant and business signage that dots the roadway.

"There's truthfully probably not one restaurant you couldn't think of that would not be off of Buford Highway," Hieu Pham once told documentarian Kate Medley, describing the road as "the international of Atlanta." In the same strip mall as Pham's own Crawfish Shack, there's Heart of India and, in the lot next door, an Ethiopian restaurant.

Opened in 1976, Havana Sandwich Shop is often considered the first immigrant-owned restaurant on Buford—timing that coincided with a wave of immigration to the South, which trended upward through the 1990s. Buford became home to many new Americans, its apartment complexes and strip malls having been emptied out by factory cutoffs and closings that began in the '60s. Sponsored by the Vietnamese Baptist Church, Pham's parents arrived from Vietnam in 1980 and moved into a building off Buford that housed a large Vietnamese population. Pham was born a few years later, at Grady Memorial Hospital downtown. "I'm a true Peach boy," he's said. "I guess I'm a southern guy."

Summer vacations introduced Pham to other parts of the South, as he traveled with the Vietnamese Baptist Church to camps and conventions that rotated locations. In Louisiana, he met a crew who quickly became his closest friends and who introduced him to po' boys, peel-and-eat shrimp, and oysters—and crawfish, featured

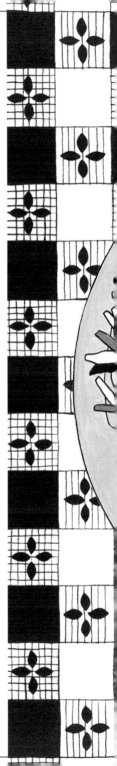

in backyard boils or simply sold out of pickup trucks along rural routes. Between events, his friends would drive to Atlanta wielding sacks of the crustaceans to prepare for Pham's family. Boiled with heavy Cajun spices and Asian aromatics like lemongrass, the dish—popular among Vietnamese communities along the Gulf Coast—formed the foundation for Pham's restaurant. He opened the Crawfish Shack in 2008 with the help of his parents and sister. In addition to his restaurant offerings, Pham stocks bags of Louisiana spice mixes and a cooler full of fresh seafood that he sells by the pound.

Crawfish and crabs are sourced from Biloxi and shrimp from the Gulf of Mexico. "My parents are both from South Vietnam, so our taste palate is more on the sweet side," he says, explaining his preference for the sweeter Gulf shrimp. "When you put them in a Cajun boil, there's a balance with the flavor." His description resonates with historians such as Tom Hanchett, who challenge the old melting pot narrative that claims immigrants lose their identities in the process of forming new ones. Instead, Hanchett describes international stretches of road like Atlanta's Buford Highway or Charlotte's Central Avenue as salad bowl suburbs, "a new, mixed-up tossed salad of cultures," where something different is created while distinct ingredients remain intact. At Pham's place, the bowl brims with spiced crawfish, corn, and potatoes—at the intersection of Vietnam, Louisiana, and Georgia.

# STANDS

Just past the flushed cheeks of Gaffney's 135-foot-tall Peachoid water tower, Abbott Farms sells South Carolina wares to travelers off I-85—peach bread, peach salsa, peach preserves, plain old peaches, and in the adjoining building, fireworks. The Peachoid Road location is one of six Abbotts outlets in the state that have roots in a rural stand that began in 1955, when the Abbott family hoped to make extra cash to buy a television. Though their aim was new, their model was well worn, as farmers had long peddled goods from roadside stands to stash supplemental cash, then known as "egg money."

"Made from salvaged lumber, burlap, and tin, no two stands were alike," writes cultural historian Dale Rosengarten, describing the ramshackle shelters that sold sweetgrass baskets and produce along South Carolina's Highway 17 in the first half of the nineteenth century. But "taken together," she adds, "they constituted an important economic engine." Stands created direct markets and provided alternatives to domestic or hourly work. It's estimated that by

the mid-1920s, tens of thousands of such shelters dotted the road. They were so abundant by 1928 that groups like the American Civic Association were hosting contests for better-looking stands in hopes of eradicating the so-called hot dog kennels—a snooty catchall term used for any roadside business selling foods perceived as cheap. But the campaign failed and the stands remained, hawking an array of mostly local goods—apples for a fried hand pie, a medley of vegetables for stewing.

For Williamson Sylvester Stuckey, it was pecans, which he began selling in 1936 from a wooden stand off Route 23 near Eastman, Georgia. Under the direction of Ethel Stuckey, the stand's offerings grew to include pralines, pecan log rolls (nuts, powdered sugar, molasses), and divinity (a nut-filled take on meringue). Stuckey's later expanded to become a fleet of full-blown buildings with teal-shingled roofs and a mynah bird or parrot that welcomed travelers at many locations—eventually some 350 stores advertised by more than four thousand billboards, which promised a free box of candy for every ten gallons of gas pumped.

Stands are starters. With little overhead and low stakes, they're often a step toward brick-and-mortar spots, a place to try something out. Though they can be found almost anywhere there's something to be sold, stands have a particular foothold in the South, where the moderate climate keeps them open almost year round. Of the thousand-plus open-air vendors, including food trucks, in Austin, Texas, many are stands. Or at least they operate as such, serving food from a walk-up window, even including "stand" in their name or description, as in the case of Las Trancas Taco Stand—a stationary metal trailer along E. Cesar Chavez Street from which al pastor and carne asada tacos are slung for a buck-fifty till midnight.

There are architectural definitions that differentiate stands from other restaurant and building types, like the "drive-in" (a structure that grew directly out of early stands) or the "outdoor walk-up" (which houses a more complex and industrialized kitchen). But none of that matters when it comes to actually dining at a stand—what scholars John A. Jakle and Keith A. Sculle deem "the most unpretentious of all eating places." It's the satisfaction of rambling up to a place like the far-flung Dip Dog Stand on Highway 11 in Marion, Virginia, where thick-battered dogs are slathered in yellow mustard and handed through a window in brown paper sacks. Owner Pam Hall has said that part of the experience is feeling slapped in the face upon opening the bag and taking a whiff of the pungent spread: a pretty good metaphor for the mighty stand, an unassuming container that surprises with its ability to pack a punch.

## EDUARDO'S TACO STAND

### OCRACOKE, NORTH CAROLINA

A tray of tacos bumps along in my bicycle basket as four of us pedal down Highway 12. We pull over near the Pony Island Motel and spread out under a tree, popping open mandarin Jarritos and swapping tortillas stuffed with marinated tuna, grilled bluefish, fried scallops, and sweet, citrus-spiked shrimp. "People from the city want fresh seafood," Eduardo Chávez tells me later. And he's right. My friends (and dog) and I have driven three hours and ferried for three more across the Pamlico Sound to be on Ocracoke, a sixteen-mile sweep of land off the North Carolina coast that Chávez calls "*the* place" for fish.

Still, when Chávez first opened his taco stand on the island in 2011, he stuck with steak and chicken, "nothing seafood." He didn't think he could compete with Ocracoke's fish basket and platter places. Nor was he convinced that the historically white village or its tourists would line up for his menu—a simple thing his daughter typed and sent from her home in Mexico City. But tastes on Ocracoke, as well as on the southern mainland, were changing. Over the course of a decade, the island's Latino population grew from 2 to 20 percent (current estimates are closer to 26). It's a significant shift for any place, but especially one whose full-time population is fewer than a thousand.

Born in Hidalgo and raised in Mexico City, Chávez left Mexico in 2002 after the stationery business he owned with his wife shuttered on the heels of a recession. He had cousins on Ocracoke and found work as a carpenter, while also stocking shelves at a gas station and bussing tables at Back Porch Restaurant. The latter led to cooking in other island kitchens. Then a metal trailer became available on the edge of the Variety Store's parking lot, providing an opportunity that didn't require a huge investment—a thing of real concern on Ocracoke, where most of the square mileage is designated as national seashore and rents are high.

There are plenty of barriers on the so-called barrier island. When Chávez began Eduardo's Taco Stand, a white man tore down the Mexican flag in front. Winters without tourists are difficult for a small business to endure. And certain ingredients are hard to come by thirty miles off the North Carolina coast. But Ocracoke is home to Chávez now. And true to the nature of the island, the highs and lows come like the tide, which he's

learned to ride out and even embrace. Chávez grows herbs and peppers in his yard to use for making salsa and garnishing local seafood, which locals and tourists increasingly request. And in the summer months, the wait for Eduardo's tacos can be upward of thirty minutes. The moveable stand has become a permanent fixture.

# TUNES

Instruments packed, A. P. Carter borrowed his brother's Essex in July of 1927 and made the winding haul from Maces Springs, Virginia, to Bristol, Tennessee, with his wife and sister-in-law in tow. The trip was likely quiet—there was no car stereo to distract them from their nerves over the recording session that awaited them down in Bristol. But within a decade, the Carter Family trio had become one of the biggest acts on the airwaves, and the Galvin brothers had built the first commercially successful in-car radio.

Folks had been trying to play music in cars for years, and the initial results were mixed. At first, there was the makeshift approach of bulky, battery-powered in-home stereos dropped onto the back seats of cars. More formal developments weren't much better. In 1922, for instance, Chevrolet fitted sedans with Westinghouse receivers, but the antenna took up most of the car's roof and the batteries couldn't be contained beneath the front seat. "It was about as convenient as taking a live orchestra along for a ride," says music writer Bill DeMain. Still, drivers with deep pockets clamored for the devices (the Westinghouse reportedly cost around $200 at a time when a whole car was about $600), wanting some of the modern conveniences experienced at home to transfer to the road.

Paul V. Galvin delivered in 1930 with his Motorola 5T71, a smaller, somewhat less expensive machine (though it still had a princely price around $130) that combined "motor" with the popular "Victrola" in its name.

Beyond the expense, a number of obstacles remained. As *Radio-Craft* magazine reported in June 1935, "Ever since auto-radio installations became popular, a controversy has been going on . . . as to whether auto radio presented an accident hazard or not." States like Connecticut proposed legislation that would enact strict fines for installing radios, which were considered distracting. But dashboard stereos buzzed on and continued to advance. In 1952, Germany's Blaupunkt manufactured the first commercially available FM car radio.

Other devices achieved varying degrees of success. In 1956, Chrysler debuted its Highway Hi-Fi, a mini turntable that slid out at the push of a button and attempted to play limited seven-inch discs produced by Columbia Records. There were obvious limitations, as records skipped on uneven roads, but there was also, for the first time, choice. Rather than listening to whatever the radio played, a driver could pick out, say, "Symphonic Serenade" by Morton Gould and the Rochester "Pops" Orchestra, or a reenactment of "The Battle of Gettysburg" (as one obviously would). Other record players followed, like the RCA Victor Auto "Victrola," which played standard 45s. "Runs as smoothly as your new car itself," an ad announced. "Designed to play over bumps, around curves or when stopping and starting." But as one might expect, the results didn't live up to the advertising, and the race was still on to create the best in-car audio player.

Robert's
WESTERN
WORLD
HOME
of
Sho~Bud
Honkytonk
Heaven
HILLBILLY
GRILL
BRAZILBILLY
HONKY TONK
GRILL
JACKS

In 1962, Earl "Madman" Muntz, a used-car and electronics salesman, launched the Muntz Stereo-Pak, which played four-track tapes and laid the groundwork for the eight-tracks that didn't skip and would soon take over. One year later, Phillips introduced cassettes, which steadily made their way into cars in the early 1970s and forever changed the sonic landscape of the American road trip. The dubbable mixtape meant a customized soundtrack for the journey or destination, later supplanted by the mix CD and the digital playlist. (The first compact-disc player was installed in a dashboard in 1984, and the iPod appeared in 2001, though it was initially difficult to connect to a car.)

The last factory-installed tape deck rolled off the line in 2010 with Lexus's SC 430, as automakers turned toward digital players and streaming services and predicted the CD's imminent decline. With all the comingand goings, it's the radio that has remained something of the King of the Road, bobbing with the ebb and flow like a hula girl doll on a dashboard.

Driving along the Crooked Road, Virginia's 330-mile musical heritage trail, WBCM 100.1 FM picks up around Bristol, where it's broadcast from the Birthplace of Country Music Museum. After launching their career in almost that very spot, the Carter Family sang it best in 1940: "There's a wonderful invention, it's called the radio," the trio warbled. "You can hear it everywhere you chance to go."

## ROBERT'S WESTERN WORLD
### NASHVILLE, TENNESSEE

Armed with a Marty Robbins box set, JesseLee Jones, a São Paulo native, unwittingly enrolled in something of a long-distance learning course on the history of country music. Weekends, he drove seven hours from his new home in Nashville, Tennessee, where he made $3 an hour scrubbing decks on the General Jackson

$2.00 ISH OF THE $6.00

RECESSION SPECIAL

Established in Milwaukee 1844

Pabst
Blue Ribbon
BEER

Showboat, to his old home in Peoria, Illinois, where he'd kept some sets playing guitar. He filled the miles with Robbins, then Little Jimmy Dickens, George Jones, and Johnny Cash, leading to what he's called his "great awakening." That rebirth eventually led him to Robert's Western World, a honkytonk on Lower Broadway.

It was 1994, and as Jones observed, "Downtown was a very different place" than it was in the 1960s, when the strip was the place to be for country musicians and their fans. The Grand Ole Opry moved out of the Ryman Auditorium—the Mother Church of country music—in the mid-'70s, making room for a string of adult bookstores and peepshows to settle in. This was the scene in the early 1990s when former boxer and veteran honkytonker Robert Wayne Moore opened Rhinestone Western Wear, a boot and apparel shop that quickly evolved.

Almost from the get-go, Moore added beer and cigarettes, then a jukebox for entertainment. To fulfill an old Alcoholic Beverage Commission law that required the sale of food along with liquor, he also implemented a menu, frying sirloin steaks and bone-in pork chop sandwiches on a small flattop grill, which differentiated his place from other bars that just offered chips. Soon after, he swapped the jukebox for live music.

"When I came down there, it was just beginning to change into a honky-tonk," Jones once told WSM radio. He later added, "The thing about it, it was real country music, too . . . I sort of found myself because I really loved that." Jones started learning more traditional country music and auditioned to play, landing the gig and earning the title of the Brazilian Hillbilly—Brazilbilly, for short.

The gig grew. In 1999, Moore retired, making Jones the heir to his so-called "Honky Tonk Heaven." That name makes sense mid-afternoon, when the bright lights of a glammed-up Broadway—a tourist destination once again—filter through a bank of storefront windows behind the stage. A band sways and sings, and the Honky Tonk Grill sizzles.

One October afternoon, a group of six or so of us, all graduate students, are enjoying a reprieve from a folklore conference down the street. We each order Jones's signature $6 Recession Special—a fried bologna sandwich with chips, a Moon Pie, and a PBR—and we stay through the next conference panel, and the next. And the next. We're on a country crash course of our own at Jones's bar. And surely, we think, there's no better teacher than the Brazilbilly and his house band.

THE RECESSION SPECIAL IS
NO BALONEY*

* BUT WITH LOTS OF BOLOGNA

# UBIQUITY

After a pilgrimage to the original McDonald's in San Bernardino, California, Matthew L. Burns hauled home broiler and milkshake machines to open Insta-Burger King in Jacksonville, Florida, with the help of a relative. After Pal Barger bumped into Ray Kroc at a restaurant convention in Illinois, then visited the first golden-arched franchise being built downstate, he beelined back to his native Appalachia to construct a burger joint named Pal's. And after Wilber Hardee drove across North Carolina, some 175 miles from Greenville to Greensboro, just to see the state's inaugural McDonald's walk-up window, he opened his own place across from East Carolina University just eleven months later.

"Probably everyone in the restaurant business began about the same time to hear stories of the new hamburger chain that served hamburgers instantly for only fifteen cents," the Hardee's founder wrote in his memoir, describing the late 1950s and early 1960s. Beyond being quick and affordable, McDonald's was splendidly modern with its slick equipment and red-and-white tiles. By design, it was also easily replicated—a chain intended to offer the same menu to folks as far apart as the east and west coasts and all points in between, which was appealing to an increasingly four-wheeled public.

Headed toward ubiquity, McDonald's franchises fanned out from Des Plaines, Illinois, with the thousandth restaurant opening well before 1970. At the same time, the Burnses and Bargers and Hardees staked out their own spots, slinging similar foods from similar-looking stands (the initial Pal's and Hardee's both incorporated red-and-white tiles). Fast food was an attractive, lucrative business, as Hardee calculated on his visit to the Greensboro McDonald's. "What impressed me was, I set out in front there and saw they took in $168 in one hour," he told a reporter for *Our State* magazine decades later. "That was big money then . . . on fifteen-cent hamburgers." In its first four months, the gross profit at Hardee's reportedly reached $9,500. Hardee bought a Lincoln Continental and a house in the country. He also took on two partners, who aimed to expand the business into new towns (and who later bought Hardee out entirely in that process).

For the most part, restaurant franchise owners tended to be young white men inclined to serve the communities most familiar to them. In the Jim Crow era, it didn't matter that the quick-service restaurants had no formal dining rooms to segregate. Franchisees set up shop in white neighborhoods, often cut off from downtown transit lines, and prioritized the folks living around them, hiring and serving those individuals first. Of course, there were also instances of blatant racism. As historian Angela Jill Cooley details in *To Live and Dine in Dixie*, three years after downtown Greensboro's lunch counters were integrated and on the heels of the Woolworth's sit-ins of 1960, the local McDonald's still denied equality: resistance included a stand-in since there was nowhere to formally sit.

In Memphis, Mahalia Jackson helped build a new kind of chicken hut—"the first national fast food franchising system under complete Negro management," the *Philadelphia Tribune* reported in 1968. "Mahalia Jackson's . . . has all the necessary features to enable the Afro-American community to take a great step forward." Bearing the activist and gospel singer's name, the chicken church (with its tall pitched roof like a steeple, and stained glass above the entrance) promised economic clout within and for African American communities. In places like Atlanta and Chicago, franchise licenses were only granted where black ownership was guaranteed at more than half. As author Alice Randall puts it, Mahalia Jackson's Chicken "gave pride back to black folk, just the way her music gave pride back to black folk on the hardest days that came."

If Harland Sanders's Kentucky Fried Chicken showed southerners that their slow foods could be quick and convenient, then patting out further proof were Jack Fulk and Mayo Boddie, two Hardee's franchisees, who put scratch-made biscuits on their North Carolina and Virginia menus in the early '70s as a means to extend business hours. Maurice Jennings of Burlington, North Carolina, had a similar notion for his regional chain. "I was on my way to our Chapel Hill Pizzaville, and it occurred to me that we could take the salad bar down at night and open the next morning with a jelly bar and freshly made buttermilk biscuits," he wrote. The first Biscuitville opened in Danville, Virginia, in 1975, and all Pizzavilles were

soon converted. The restaurant's sign was not a yellow arch but a golden rolling pin. And after it went up, a battering of biscuit drive-thrus followed.

# MILO'S HAMBURGERS
## BIRMINGHAM, ALABAMA

There's trepidation on the telephone line. "You've been here before?" asks Mary Duncan Proctor, marketing manager for Milo's Hamburgers in Alabama. "Many times," I tell her, and she seemingly relaxes, knowing that we speak the same language. The vernacular here is Milo's signature sauce, which is difficult to sum up. "A lot of people call it gravy," Proctor says in her Alabama accent. "A lot of people call it barbecue sauce. It's obviously neither of those."

The closest condiment is A-1. But Milo's sauce has more heft. The joint's success has hinged on the goopy stuff since Milo's opened in Birmingham's Northside in 1946. As the legend goes, Milo Carlton, a mess-hall cook during World War II, asked his early patrons to provide input into the sauce he fiddled with each day, until he landed on the current recipe. Birmingham then ate it up. The city has an affinity for sauces, including the chili-esque fixin that finishes its hot dogs at Greek institutions like Gus's.

In the 1990s, at the behest of Carlton's neighbor Dean Chitwood, Milo's began to spread out (there are now fourteen scattered in and around Birmingham). But when the restaurant tried to leave town, the sauce created a mess. The burger is befuddling "if you think you're about to eat barbecue sauce," Proctor warns about a widespread misconception. The comparison "is like saying that ranch is honey mustard. It's just not."

Only two people at Milo's reportedly know the ingredients. "I am not one of them," Proctor says. What she knows is that its cooking process takes six hours, with a very specific order to the steps. As in making mayonnaise, adding one thing before another can have disastrous results. It's not unlike the process of building a local chain restaurant—there's a specific process. The first Milo's franchises were a flop, all shuttering as the company failed to explain one of its only offerings to outsiders. "It's a love-it-or-hate-it burger," says Proctor. "You either loved it or hated it and moved on."

But in the past five years, Milo's has successfully grown beyond Birmingham into cities like Tuscaloosa. The strategy included offering an option the menu calls "Burgers—The Other Way" (no Milo's Sauce) and chicken, as well as an extended line of sauces that includes Boom Boom (described as "smooth with heat") and plain old honey mustard. Essentially, Milo's has expanded its vocabulary, while proudly hanging on to its original accent.

# V

# VACANCY

Piped out in 836 feet of neon tubing and towering nearly 43 feet high, the Holiday Inn's Great Sign lit up the road in 1952, beckoning drivers off of Memphis's Summer Avenue, and, soon after, three other entrances to the city. By the mid-1960s, close to 500 locations spanned the United States and Montreal. As the Great Sign's marquee often touted, Kemmons Wilson's motel had become "The World's Innkeeper," offering quality and consistency along the highway.

Wilson had found neither a year earlier, en route to DC with his wife and five kids. "In short, it was a miserable trip," he recalled. A rate of $6 quickly became $16 when a motel charged $2 extra per child, sending Wilson back to Memphis determined to open a place where children could stay with their parents for free. Beyond that deal, his Holiday Inns featured a swimming pool, air conditioning, childcare, free ice, a telephone in every room, ample parking, and a dog kennel. The Holiday Inn's amenities were vastly different from those of the Peabody, a hotel in downtown Memphis that broadcast the music of swing orchestras to southern listeners in the 1940s from its elegant Skyway ballroom.

Luxury hotels like the Peabody were (and still are) largely located in compact downtowns, which were convenient to those traveling by rail but difficult for drivers, who had to navigate parking. In addition, rooms were priced high, and social expectations set even higher, as guests donned their finest attire for formal dinners. This would have been especially difficult in the early days of automobile travel when guests, having traveled rough roads with open (or no) windows, often checked in under a thin layer of dust and were expected to be cleaned up and presentable by the dinner hour. Partially in reaction, a freewheeling movement caught on in the 1920s, as tourists packed everything they might need into their cars and took off, camping at night wherever the road led them—a small shoulder, a patch of farm, a sprawling field.

In the end, comfort beat out rugged self-reliance, and a slew of businesses sprouted up to offer roadside rest, from designated stops like the Dixie Tourist Camp in Kingstree, South Carolina, that advertised "comfortable cabins in a beautiful grove of hickory and oaks," to mom-and-pop operations. Independently owned motels were convenient and, compared to hotels, cheap—of particular benefit during the Great Depression. Focusing on a traveler's basic necessities, the fairly uncomplicated businesses afforded opportunities for families living along rural routes to

make extra income. In 1951, Lon and Annie Loveless fried chicken and patted out biscuits to sate drivers along Highway 100 near Nashville, eventually constructing a fourteen-room motel—the venerable Loveless Motel and Café (now just a restaurant).

After World War II, the members of a new leisure class found themselves with higher incomes and living standards, and many mom-and-pop motels had a hard time keeping up. Kemmons Wilson hit upon something of a solution. He franchised his Holiday Inns, which combined some of a hotel's comforts with a motel's conveniences, all at an affordable price. The Great Sign quickly became a symbol of reliability on the road, as did the sunburst of Atlanta's Days Inns and the lamplighter characters on the first franchised Howard Johnson motel, located in Savannah.

But the Great Sign hardly meant great things for all. In the Jim Crow South, vacancy lights dimmed for travelers of color. "Our bodies, heavy with the fatigue of travel, cannot gain lodging in the motels of the highways and the hotels of the cit-

ies," Martin Luther King Jr. called out across the National Mall in 1963, and public lodgings became major battlegrounds for civil rights. On June 18, 1964, James Brock poured acid into a swimming pool of protesters at the Monson Motor Lodge in St. Augustine, Florida. A day later, the Civil Rights Act was passed in the Senate.

Many of the events in the continued fight for civil rights were organized by traveling activists at black-owned spaces like the Lorraine Motel. Just South of Beale Street in Memphis, Walter and Loree Bailey's lodge was listed in the *Negro Motorist Green Book* and also became a preferred hub for musicians, including Ray Charles and Aretha Franklin, who recorded nearby. "We'd go down to the Lorraine Motel and we'd lay by the pool and Mr. Bailey would bring us fried chicken and we'd eat ice cream," Issac Hayes recalled. "We'd just frolic until the sun goes down and [then] we'd go back to work."

Since 1991, the motel has housed the National Civil Rights Museum. A white wreath hangs on the balcony in front of the teal door of Room 306, near the spot where Martin Luther King Jr. was assassinated in 1968. Inside, the contents of his room are displayed just as they were left that April day—a cup of coffee on the dresser, a newspaper spread across the bed. "I am tired, I am weak, I am worn," Mahalia Jackson's voice sings from a speaker in the motel's hallway. "Through the storm, through the night, lead me on through the light."

## THUNDERBIRD INN

### SAVANNAH, GEORGIA

A "d" flickers on the Thunderbird's neon sign at the advertised "INTERSECTION OF YES MA'AM & DUDE." Mark Thomas, the innkeeper, motions to the marquee. "You want to come across as the epitome of southern charm," he says, "but you also want that California edge." California lays claim to the first-named "motel" with San Luis Obispo's Milestone Motel (called The Motel Inn by locals), built in 1925, but Savannah, Georgia, played a major role in standardizing such roadside units. It's where Howard Deering Johnson, already known for some four hundred orange-roofed restaurants, built his first motor lodge in 1954.

The Thunderbird Inn opened off US 17 ten years later and flourished into the early 1970s. Then it went the way of many motels, which were being skirted by a burgeoning interstate system, and fell into a dark state

Thunderbird
Inn

AT
INTERSECTION
OF
YES MA'AM
& DUDE

of disrepair that even its highlighter-yellow paint job couldn't brighten. "There were pine trees growing through the sign," says Thomas, who helped Bill O'Brien reopen the building in the early 2000s. They began with the exterior, installing red, teal, and yellow tile panels. But inside, Thomas says the redo "looked like a Hampton Inn."

Now revamped inside and out, all forty-two rooms are outfitted with mid-century modern furniture and fixtures. There are faux rotary phones by the bed, and '60s songs piped through the balcony's speakers. In this, the Thunderbird joins motels like the Mother Earth Motor Lodge of Kinston, North Carolina, in reselling "retro" in the guise of a modern boutique. Thomas catalogs such spots on a website called Travel Retro, which he manages with his wife. "You *can* travel and vacation without staying in the same bland hotel room, coast to coast," it asserts. And the Thunderbird proves the point.

When we arrive, there are Moon Pies on the bed, RC Colas on the nightstand, and the next morning, coffee and Krispy Kreme doughnuts in the lobby. "All of that was just to lean into the retro and embrace things that are old and southern and classic," Thomas explains. But the appeal of the Thunderbird is that it's not completely stuck in time. The motel strives to be green, outfitted with an impressive number of solar panels, and is welcoming to travelers of all backgrounds. "You think of this old building, it's cinderblock," says Thomas, "and you think, 'What can we do to it for the future?'" The answer lies both within and beyond the enameled walls.

# W

# WINDOWS

Brookie Pool opened the Toot-N-Tell restaurant in 1946 with an attractive concept: customers could drive up, toot their horn, and tell a carhop their order. The name was less appealing to Pool's granddaughter, Donna Sparkman. At school she was chided as heir to the Poot-N-Smell-It. But the idea worked. People came in droves to get carryout from the restaurant in Garner, North Carolina. "Who can forget the stupid name?" asks Sparkman, who now runs the place.

In the late '50s, the Toot-N-Tell followed the lead of many drive-ins, adding a drive-up window. Now a mainstay on the road, the drive-thru is thought to have originated in 1931 at Pig Stand No. 21, a California franchise of a Texas-based drive-in founded by Jesse G. Kirby and Dr. Reuben Jackson. At the Pig Stand, customers placed orders for Tennessee-style barbecue sandwiches at the same window where their orders were filled. "There are plenty of other firsts attributed to them too: the first onion ring, the first chicken-fried steak sandwich, Texas toast, neon lights. Some of those claims may be hard to prove," writes Daniel Vaughn, *Texas Monthly*'s barbecue editor, "but they all serve as anecdotal evidence of Kirby and Jackson's innovativeness."

Early drive-up windows were all about trial and error. At California's Jack in the Box, arguably the first major chain to install windows, timing was a thing to be fine-tuned. The restaurant reportedly needed three minutes to serve a line of four cars. So to allow for proper prep time, they situated a microphone three car-lengths from the pick-up window, and also toyed with sending employees out to cars with microphones. John Galardi implemented one of the wackiest window experiments, designing an A-frame with a drive-thru that cut through the middle of the building at Der Wienerschnitzel, another California chain. But it was Dave Thomas, formerly employed by Kentucky Fried Chicken, who made perhaps the boldest move. Thomas placed a drive-up window on the first stand-alone Wendy's in 1971, and then at every location that followed.

As Philip Langdon details in the history of drive-thrus in *Orange Roofs, Golden Arches*, by the end of the decade, Wendy's made approximately 46 percent of its sales at the window. "Watching the success of this upstart competitor, McDonald's, Burger King, and others belatedly knocked holes in the walls of their own restaurants and installed drive-thru windows,"

Langdon writes. Some, like Checker's in Mobile, Alabama, and Rally's in Louisville, Kentucky (now merged under one umbrella), knocked two holes in their walls to create double drive-thrus in the mid 1980s, handing out burgers left and right.

In 2016, Americans placed 12.4 billion drive-up orders, accounting for between 60 and 70 percent of revenue at quick-service restaurants. Drive-thrus continue to innovate and create new gimmicks, including separate payment windows, touchscreens, and ordering apps, as they respond to this window-reliant world. It's like the voice that crackles through the drive-thru's speaker often puts it: "Next window, please."

## PAL'S SUDDEN SERVICE

### KINGSPORT, TENNESSEE

We approach the drive-thru window at Pal's wielding a stopwatch. "Go," my friend Ashley calls out, which really signals me to stop. Sixteen seconds later, we pull away from the window with a sack of Pal's signature Sauceburgers and Frenchie Fries. We eat them in the car, parked in the shadow of the humongous hot dog and hamburger sculptures affixed to the restaurant.

Apparently, those oversized lunchables didn't impress the *Harvard Business Review*, which reported in a 2016 profile, "At first blush, there's nothing all that amazing about Pal's." Instead, what inspired the reporter was the restaurant's "lightning pace." "Nothing about Pal's is standard for its business, or any business," the author argued. "The most obvious difference is its fanatical devotion to speed and accuracy."

According to Thom Crosby, CEO of Pal's Sudden Service, the small chain is at least three times as fast as its best competitor, delivering hamburgers to idling customers in about eighteen seconds during the lunch rush. "We look at when the wheels stop at the pick-up window to

when they start moving again," he says. In an office off Executive Park Boulevard in Kingsport, Crosby sketches a typical drive-thru line on a yellow legal pad. The only decor in the room is the bookshelf behind him, which includes Stephen R. Covey's *The 7 Habits of Highly Effective People* and Danny Meyer's *Setting the Table* and represents something of the structured side of Pal's. In addition to speed, the chain is known for its freakish accuracy (one mistake out of every 3,600 orders) and low turnover (about one third of the industry's average when it comes to line workers). "If you watch professional athletes, everything they do looks so smooth and fluid," Crosby told the *Harvard Business Review*. "But eventually you realize how much work went into that performance, all the train-ing, all the skill-building, all the hours. It's the same for us." The chain trains and retrains as part of an intensive certification program for employees.

Pal's takes its name from Pal Barger, a Kingsport native whose parents owned a bar-becue stand in town. Originally dismayed by the idea of restaurant work, Barger changed his mind in the early 1950s when he hap-pened upon 2-J, a hamburger joint in Austin, Texas, where he was stationed in the air force. Impressed by 2-J's volume and speed (a glitzy sign announced "Over 6 million sold"), Barger attended the National Restaurant Convention in Chicago, where a guy named Ray Kroc overheard him talking about hamburgers and invited him down to Des Plaines, Illinois, to see what would be-come the first McDonald's franchise.

Barger set out to do something similar in his own corner of Appalachia, constructing his first burger joint in 1956 (there are now twenty-nine Pal's locations in Southwest Virginia and East Tennessee). But he did it his own way. In the mid-1980s, the business began opening its signature drive-thrus: teal tile buildings adorned with gigantic fast-food sculptures designed by his friends, the Pop artists Karen and Tony Barone. The buildings reflect the goofier side of Pal's—the laidback version that says "Frenchie fry" or "peachy tea," that doesn't count the seconds it takes to get a chili bun but that's still glad when it's handed through the window in no time.

# XXX

The stretch where Highway 421 reaches toward the blue-tipped mountains of Watauga County, North Carolina, is known as Junior Johnson Highway—a designation that recognizes the legendary NASCAR driver who won a total of fifty races over his career. In these parts, however, Johnson was as famous for his long tenure running moonshine over in neighboring Wilkes County. He was fourteen when he started driving liquor for his father, who, in 1935, was arrested when agents found 7,100 gallons of whiskey at his place in Ingle Hollow.

Illegal booze has long been linked with driving. As Tammy Ingram puts it in *Dixie Highway*, Prohibition "depended on good roads as much as fast cars." The Midwest-to-South corridor was notoriously called "Avenue de Booze" and "Rummers' Runway," as bootleggers moved whiskey southward out of Canada. Even after Prohibition was repealed, many counties remained dry and federal taxes on alcohol were high, creating a profitable market for

bootleggers like Percy Flowers of Johnston County, North Carolina. As Johnson recalls, a runner could make up to $450 a night speeding down back roads to deliver booze during the 1950s (the equivalent of around $4,700 today).

To outpace the law, bootleggers often bolstered their Ford V8s. Though stock car racing can trace its beginnings to the white sands of Daytona Beach, it came into its own in the red-clay Piedmont, where working-class men pushed new speeds in the 1930s. "There [were] a lot of bootlegging people involved when racing got off the ground," Johnson once told producer David Padrusch. "And if anything boosted it and made it successful I would think you have to give the bootlegging people a big, big part of the credit for it."

Clearly, not all stock car drivers became as successful as Junior Johnson, nor did all the runners have his luck. In the mid-'80s, Presdient Reagan pardoned him for his 1956 conviction for distilling moonshine with his dad's old still. And today he's gone legal, making Midnight Moon corn whiskey as a part owner of Piedmont Distillers. Similarly, other distilleries have begun capitalizing on the name of old-time shiners like Popcorn Sutton or Doc Collier, legally producing whiskey under new laws. In 2009, the State General Assembly of Tennessee made distilling lawful in forty-one counties (previously, it was legit in only three). The result was an increase in whiskey-soaked tourism. As folklorist Graham Hoppe has observed, "moonshine has become as much a tourist draw as the Ferris wheels and wax museums" along Gatlinburg and

Pigeon Forge's Parkway. At one spot on the highway, a jug-shaped sign inscribed XXX—shorthand for booze—invites drivers into Doc Collier's tasting room. Half a mile further, a Ripley's sign sums up the wonder of now-legal shine at the foot of the Great Smokies: Believe It or Not.

## HARRODSBURG, KENTUCKY

With sixteen distilleries on the Kentucky Bourbon Trail and with limited time in the Bluegrass State, we collapse with indecision at Harrodsburg's Beaumont Inn. It quickly becomes clear we've made a good decision. Located on the Inn's rolling acreage, the Old Owl Tavern counts upward of 120 bourbon labels among its offerings. Plus, there's the promise of a two-year-old ham, yellow-leg fried chicken, corn pudding, and cornbread in the dining room—what Duncan Hines once proclaimed "the best eating place in Kentucky."

The Beaumont's main house, constructed in 1845, was used as a women's school under several different names. Then, around 1917, Glave and Annie Bell Goddard purchased the building and transitioned it to an inn. A graduate of the school, Annie Bell taught mathematics there and later became Beaumont's dean—first of the school, then of her very own dining room, where she entertained former alums and their families. The Goddards prepared a one-year ham, which they aged an additional year on their property, and yellow-legged chickens, considered a premium breed by some. ("The yellow leg business is a nonsensical fancy," the American Poultry Advocate grumbled in 1912.) But the Goddards didn't serve a drop of (legal) alcohol. Prohibition laws hung around Mercer County, Kentucky, much longer than they did in other places.

Then in 2003, Harrodsburg passed a local option ordinance, which allowed Beaumont to acquire a liquor license. The timing coincided

# XXX

# GOOD LEGS!

KENTUCKY
OWL BOURBON →

↓ YELLOW-LEGGED
FRIED CHICKEN

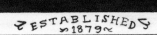

THE WISE MAN'S
BOURBON

KENTUCKY OWL

KENTUCKY
STRAIGHT
BOURBON
WHISKEY

750 ML

FOUNDER
C. M. DEDMAN

BOTTLED IN
...DSTOWN, KY    60.5

with Dixon Dedman's graduation from Wofford College, so Annie Bell's grandson returned to Beaumont to carve out his own place in the family business, drawing on an extensive knowledge of Kentucky mash. "It's a passion of mine," says Dedman. "It's been a passion of mine for longer than I might admit in front of my mother."

Dedman comes by it honestly. Before Prohibition, his great-great-grandfather, C. M. Dedman, distilled, bottled, and sold Kentucky Owl Bourbon in North Mercer County. Then, as family lore goes, federal agents seized 250,000 gallons in 1916, shipping it up to a Frankfort warehouse for storage, where the liquor supposedly fueled a fire (some surmise it was actually sent further, up to Chicago to fuel the speakeasies of Al Capone). That was that until 2014, when Dedman began distilling a new bourbon blend, revived under the name Kentucky Owl Straight Bourbon Whiskey. "It's been a neat way for us to connect with our guests," says Dedman, "to sit down with them and drink bourbon." In a tumbler, it's all neat, indeed—and it's just a few steps up to bed.

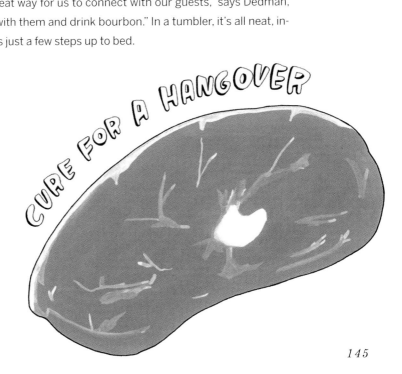

CURE FOR A HANGOVER

# YONDER

As one of Will Harris's regular sayings goes, "It's a journey and not a destination." But the fourth-generation cattleman at White Oak Pastures knows that for rural outposts like his, it's actually a bit of both. Taking US 27 through southwestern Georgia, it's a haul to get to White Oak Pastures, but it's worth the drive—to behold 3,000 acres of organic farmland, to eat a hamburger in the farm's open-air pavilion, or just to buy a roll of toilet paper. "It is literally in the middle of nowhere," Harris's daughter, Jenni, says of their home in Bluffton, Georgia, a community that counted 103 residents in the 2010 census. Then she checks off the closest shops— eighty miles to a mall, fifty to a Target, fifteen to a grocery, and ten to a gas station. When Will Harris was a kid, Bluffton was long past its heyday. Still, there was a dry goods store, a meat market, and two general stores.

Founded in 1866, White Oak Pastures grew up alongside the country store, a marketplace that proliferated after the Civil War and became the front porch for a changing region. "From 1865 to 1930, no institution influenced the South's economy, politics, and the daily life of its people more than the crossroads store," sociologist Edgar T. Thompson once wrote. Country stores were accessible one-stop shops for communities isolated by the South's then impassable roads, stocking everything from clothes to medicines to seeds to food. In doing so, they built a bridge to other places—offering goods from both near and far—and provided a hangout for neighbors. Thompson argued that while churches and schools remained seg-regated for a century more, "There was an air of familiarity and tolerance at the store rarely matched elsewhere." But "rarely matched" remains too positive: black and Native southerners still suffered indignities—and sometimes injuries, and worse—in the Jim Crow era, as Emmett Till's visit to Bryant's Grocery & Meat Market grimly underscored in 1955.

COUNTRY STORE CATCHALL

CRICKET →

↗CRACKER

STEEL SHOT →

By the end of World War I, general stores began to shutter en masse as new cars traveled better roads to other marketplaces and opportunities, including increasingly popular chains—though some stores located on the outskirts of towns were able to hang on. And so it was that by the late 1960s, no mercantiles remained in Bluffton. "Between 1968 and 2016, there was nowhere to purchase anything," says Jenni Harris. Then Will Harris made an offer for Herman Bass's old general store, long aban-doned, its shelves still lined with rusting cans of Pee Wee's Early June Peas and Sunshine's Pork and Beans. Harris had no intention of reopening the shop, but heavier traffic on US 27—which had expanded from two to four lanes—put pressure on White Oak Pastures to offer something more.

The White Oak Pastures General Store is committed to supplying mostly farm or Georgia-made goods. "We don't want to feel like a Wal-Mart," Jenni jokes. But there's still an all-in-oneness to it that's typical of remaining (or revamped) crossroads stores. "We always call us a mini Wal-Mart," Levern Darby once told South Carolina public television, de-scribing Cooper's Country Store, where he slow cooks barbecue. "You see,

# THE STICKS OUT YONDER

it's a rural area, and there were no other stores around back in the day." Cooper's, which opened near Salters, South Carolina, in 1937, contains a seemingly endless stock: cast-iron frying pans, steel shot, crickets, crackers, liver pudding, and home-cured country hams. "The other day I had an old man come in here looking for a shovel handle. He had been three or four other places and couldn't find one," third-generation owner Russell Cooper once told *Garden & Gun* magazine. "Well, I had it."

Today's rural general stores often service travelers who find themselves between destinations or who seek out remote experiences. Off-the-beaten-path is part of the appeal, as is the hunt for authenticity. That can be played up, in the manner of a Cracker Barrel Country Store, to service a nostalgic notion, often crystallized in the form of old-fashioned candy. But to survive and remain relevant out yonder, the crossroads store also has to intersect with real needs—as small as a fishing hook, as big and wide as the front porch for a whole community.

## JEFFERSON COUNTRY STORE
### JEFFERSON, ALABAMA

The Jefferson Country Store shelves all the standards: Little Debbies and Chef Boyardee, cold beer and BC Powder, Duracells and Tide. In its remote corner of Marengo County, Alabama, it sort of has to. It's the only gas station, pharmacy, and grocery for ten miles in any direction. Before it opened, "you were at least fifteen minutes away from a roll of toilet paper," says Betsy Compton, who owns the business with her partner Tony Luker.

The store, which has gone by a few different names since it opened in 1957, closed for a year in 2012 when Betsy's Aunt Hattie retired. "It

felt like a big part of our community was dwindling," says Betsy. "It was hurting us not to have our store." So she and Tony called around trying to find someone to take it on. When that proved futile, they reopened it themselves. Tony had experience in beverage sales, and Betsy knew public relations (she still works in PR for the University of West Alabama in Livingston). But what made them a particularly good fit was their knowledge of the place and people. "I grew up in here," says Betsy. "This is just where we were. We didn't go to daycare."

In 2013, a month after the doors reopened, the town of Demopolis absorbed the zip code of unincorporated Jefferson, nullifying the need for the post office that had operated inside the store for almost four decades. "That's sort of a hard pill for us to swallow," says Betsy. "We're trying to get Jefferson on the map to stay." Part of the strategy now includes Tony's homemade chicken salad and pimento cheese, smoked pigtails, a hot ham and cheese sandwich, and Betsy's caramel cake, which is sold by the slice. "People aren't going to come from Demopolis just to get a bag of chips," she says.

On a Tuesday in mid-August, I make a wide swing west en route to Florida to eat with Betsy and Tony at a table in the middle of the store. Lunch is thick-cut rag bologna, charred black, draped in hoop cheese and bundled between two pieces of toast. It's the day of the Democratic primary, and people stream in talking about everything from the polls to childcare to cold beer in the cooler. "We reopened because we live here and wanted to support the community," Betsy says. Later, back on the road, the radio is abuzz over how to unite a divided Alabama. A seat at Jefferson's long table seems like a start.

# Z

## ZEALOTS

At Prince's Hot Chicken in Nashville, women have been known to roll on the floor. Men have jumped up and tap-danced across the tables. And a few escapades have been reported in the parking lot. "Yes," André Prince Jeffries has confirmed, "some strange things go on associated with hot chicken." It's true that the chicken chapel attracts an unusual band of zealots, who fall in line on Fridays and Saturdays until midnight to succumb to its fiery meats. But folks have done even weirder things in the name of a humble donut.

In the case of Nashville's hot chicken, which started with Thornton Prince in the 1930s, there's an addictive quality to the spices—a cayenne-induced fever that releases endorphins and creates a certain high. It's part

HOT DONUTS

of what keeps townies coming back day after day. But there's also a larger draw, part of which is the social cachet one gets from living to tell the tale through burning lips. "Food is one of the most popular things people talk about," Jonah Berger, author of *Contagious: Why Things Catch On*, once told a reporter—and the extreme dish or singular experience makes for a good story.

Spread by word of mouth (or the mouthpiece of social media), stories increase the hype of specific foods or places (Jeffries says Prince's hasn't advertised in about twenty years). It's the same reason a line attracts more people to the line. People are apt to join in to see what the buzz is about, particularly when there's a treat at the end. Psychologists who research waiting—the formal field of study is called queuing theory—have

found that individuals are willing to stand twice as long in a line for food as they are for anything else. At Britt's Donuts in Carolina Beach, that could easily mean two hours.

It sounds frivolous, and it is, because fun is part of the attraction. But underneath the donut's glaze, or the chicken's spices, there's real substance. A true zealot isn't made without the conviction that some thing, or some place, matters. In the case of hot chicken, KFC exported it to a national market in 2016. Still, people line up at Prince's and Nashville's other hot chicken joints. The city even puts on a festival devoted to the blistering bird. In Nashville's restaurants, or at its events, customers swap stories and survival tips—regular is hot, milk helps. They talk about where they've come from, or why they've come here. And they eat chicken. Maybe they roll around. Maybe they dance.

## FRANKLIN BARBECUE
### AUSTIN, TEXAS

It's dead quiet on Austin's East 11th Street. The morning finds Aaron Franklin standing in line down the road at Figure 8 Coffee—for the second time since 9 a.m. "You're back," the barista greets him when we make our way to the front. It's nothing new for Franklin, the seasoned pitmaster of Franklin Barbecue, to be up early. But mornings generally place him near a line of his own making—one hundreds of people deep, snaking around his barbecue joint and up the adjacent street.

In late August of 2017, one person was reportedly already in line when a fire truck arrived at Franklin's a little before 5:30 a.m. (the restaurant opens at 11 a.m.). A spark had caught in the pitroom behind a rotisserie smoker named Bethesda. Now, two months later, Franklin, wearing a T-shirt that depicts David Bowie as a cat, appears calm—despite double caffeination—as he talks about using the forced downtime to make improvements to the restaurant's building. He's been fidgeting with smokers since dawn.

Franklin Barbecue opened in December 2009, just a white-and-aqua trailer on a friend's empty lot. An urban joint in East Austin that spiked its sauce with espresso, Franklin's had its skeptics. Then word of its supposedly life-changing brisket started to spread, and the line started forming. "I looked out one day and there were about five people outside the fence. The next day there were seven, then nine," says Franklin. "At that point I thought it was bizarre. I still think it's bizarre."

Barbecue stokes fanaticism. People make pilgrimages to commune at Smitty's or Louie Mueller or Southside Market in central Texas for sausages and smoked brisket. In the town of Bryan, Franklin's father owned a joint, where Franklin worked in middle school, slicing onions and lemons. The restaurant was short-lived, but it laid the foundation. Franklin began experimenting with brisket on a backyard smoker in his twenties, hosting parties with his wife (and now business partner), Stacy, to test his skills. The results attracted a new level of barbecue zealot.

Folks wait hours for a tray of Franklin's peppered brisket. And they don't do so idly. They unfold chairs, spread out blankets, read books, play Monopoly, drink coffee, slug beer. "A lot of people show up and expect to have a good time," says Franklin. "It's actually turned into its own tailgate." Franklin sends out snacks and keeps up with what people plan to order through a complex system (walkie-talkies and a designated line monitor included), sometimes selling out before the doors actually open. "We make loose calculations," he says, "kind of like when you grade a cow before slaughter."

With all the waiting, Franklin claims he's never fielded a complaint. "A cool thing about the line is that it filters out cranky people," he says (a

statement that resonates with scholars who study lines). Fans are in it for the long haul, including the couple of months the fire put the pit on pause. "The outpouring of love has been insane," he says, finishing up his coffee. A month later, when the joint reopens, the line starts forming at 2:00 a.m.

# ACKNOWLEDGMENTS

For their help on this book, I'm indebted to many fine friends and colleagues, who provided invaluable feedback, and, in many cases, also joined me on the road or for a meal: Katy Clune, Amy Evans, Bill Ferris, Anna Hamilton, Emily Hilliard, Christina Lajunesse, Kate Medley, Ashley Melzer, Sara Camp Milam, Travis Proffitt, Lora Smith, Sara Roahen, Daniel Wallace, and Sara Wood. I'm also grateful to Marcie Cohen Ferris and John T. Edge, whose good work always sets the standard, and to the folks at the Southern Foodways Alliance, whose resources and support were essential.

A huge thanks is due to the Center for the Study of the American South, which funded research and travel, and to all of my colleagues there, who kept me afloat with their good humor and better advice. In particular, Ayse Erginer read and offered comments on multiple drafts of the manuscript (drawings, too!), and, along with Emma Calabrese, helped carry the weight of *Southern Cultures*.

I couldn't ask for a better editor than Casey Kittrell—a brilliant collaborator and friend—or for a better team than everyone at UT Press, especially Lynne Chapman and Dustin Kilgore. I'm also grateful for the keen eye and sharp wit of designer Amanda Weiss, and to the readers who provided comments on the manuscript.

This book wouldn't be possible without my mother's long champion-ing of my creative works. I'm thankful for her encouragement, which in this case included hopping in the car with me for research-related travel. And a ginormous thanks to Land Arnold, who supported me daily during this entire process, and who provided thoughtful feedback as a partner, bookseller, and fellow road food enthusiast—here's to thousands of miles, and counting.

Portions of this book were written at the Weymouth Center for the Arts, Wild Acres, and at small cottages in Damascus, Virginia, and Ocracoke Island, North Carolina, accompanied by Rubick the dog.

# SOURCES

## ARCHITECTURE

Berry, Lee. Interview with the author, June 27, 2017, Ellerbe, North Carolina.

Gebhard, David. "Programmatic Architecture: An Introduction." *SCA Journal* 13.2 (1995): 2–7.

Hinnant, Kristy Hill. Phone conversation with the author, July 5, 2017.

Kazek, Kelly. *Forgotten Tales of Alabama*. Charleston, SC: The History Press, 2010.

Klinkenberg, Jeff. "Canned sunshine, anyone?" *St. Petersburg Times*, January 7, 2007.

*A Program About Unusual Buildings & Other Roadside Stuff*. PBS, produced by Rick Sebak and WQED. Multimedia Pittsburgh, September 22, 2011.

Venturi, Robert, Denise Scott Brown, and Steven Izenour. *Learning from Las Vegas: The Forgotten Symbolism of Architectural Form*, rev. ed. Cambridge, MA: MIT Press, 1977.

## BILLBOARDS

*Billboard Advertising*, vol. 1, no. 1 (Cincinnati), November 1, 1894, accessed via the Internet Archive, https://ia800307.us.archive.org/21/items/billboard01-1894/billboard01-1894.pdf.

Gudis, Catherine. *Buyway: Billboards, Automobiles, and the American Landscape*. New York: Routledge, 2004.

King, P. Nicole. *Sombreros and Motorcycles in a Newer South: The Politics of Aesthetics in South Carolina's Tourism Industry*. Jackson: University of Mississippi Press, 2012.

Kuntz, Tom. "Word for Word/Billboards from God; Did Somebody Say, 'Give Me a Sign, Lord'?" *New York Times*, July 18, 1999, https://www.nytimes.com/1999/07/18/weekinreview/word-for-word-billboards-from-god-did-somebody-say-give-me-a-sign-lord.html.

Wallace, Emily. "Cult Soda and Soft-Core Porn in Imaginary Mexico," *PUNCH*, July 22, 2014, https://punchdrink.com/articles/cult-soda-soft-core-porn-in-imaginary-mexico/.

### CARS

Dean, Sam. "The History of the Cup Holder." *Bon Appétit*, February 18, 2013.

Jakle, John A., and Keith A. Sculle. *Fast Food: Roadside Restaurants in the Automobile Age*. Baltimore, MD: Johns Hopkins University Press, 1999.

Johnson, Charlie, and Jonathan Walker. "Peak Car Ownership Report," 2016. Rocky Mountain Institute, https://rmi.org/insight/peak-car-ownership-report/.

Johnson, Dave. "With Hat on Head, He Hops to It." *Los Angeles Times*, October 11, 1987, http://articles.latimes.com/1987-10-11/news/mn-13508_1_trademark-hats.

McKay, Dave. Phone conversation with the author, May 21, 2018.

US Department of Transportation, Federal Highway Administration. *Highway Statistics: Summary to 1985*, Table MV-201. Washington, DC: US Government Printing Office, n.d..

US Department of Transportation, Federal Highway Administration. *Selected Highway Statistics and Charts, 1990*, Table ss90-4, ss90-17. Washington, DC: US Government Printing Office, n.d.

White, E. B. "Farewell, My Lovely!" *New Yorker*, May 16, 1936.

Wilson, Charles Reagan. *The New Encyclopedia of Southern* Culture, Vol. 4: Myth, Manners, & Memory. Chapel Hill: University of North Carolina Press, 2004.

## DIRECTIONS

Dawson, Carol, and Roger Allen Polson. *Miles and Miles of Texas: 100 Years of the Texas Highway Department*. College Station: Texas A&M University Press, 2016.

Dodd, David. Interview with the author, August 16, 2017, Tallahassee, Florida.

*The Green Book*. New York: Victor H. Green & Co., 1937–1967. Accessed via the Schomburg Center for Research in Black Culture, The New York Public Library Digital Collections, https://digitalcollections.nypl.org/collections/the-green-book#/?tab=about&scroll=15.

Hines, Duncan. *Adventures in Good Eating: Good Eating Places Along the Highways and in Cities of America*, 27th printing. Bowling Green, KY: Adventures in Good Eating, Inc., 1945.

Ingram, Tammy. *Dixie Highway: Road Building and the Making of the Modern South, 1900–1930*. Chapel Hill: University of North Carolina Press, 2014.

Road Map Collectors Association. *The Legend*. Accessed via roadmaps.org.

Stager, Claudette, and Martha Carver, eds. *Looking Beyond the Highway: Dixie Roads and Culture*. Knoxville: University of Tennessee Press, 2006.

"Ties to Texas." In *Texas Transportation Researcher*, Vol. 41, No. 4 (2005), https://static.tti.tamu.edu/tti.tamu.edu/documents/researcher/ttr-v41-n4.pdf.

## ENTERTAINMENT

Bly, Lauren. "Hooray for Dollywood: Tennessee. theme park celebrates 25th anniversary." *USA Today*, May 25, 2010, http://usatoday30.usatoday.com/travel/destinations/2010-05-20-dollywood-anniversary-N.htm.

Cox, Victoria. Interview with the author, August 17, 2017, Weeki Wachee Springs, Florida.

Hollis, Tim. *Dixie Before Disney: 100 Years of Roadside Fun*. Jackson: University Press of Mississippi, 1999.

Rabinovitz, Lauren. *Electric Dreamland: Amusement Parks, Movies, and American Modernity*. New York: Columbia Unversity Press, 2012.

Revels, Tracy J. *Sunshine Paradise: A History of Florida Tourism*. Gainesville: University Press of Florida, 2011.

## FIXINS

Evans, Amy. "Gus Koutroulakis Oral History," Birmingham, Alabama, March 8–9, 2004. Southern Foodways Alliance, https://www.southernfoodways .org/app/uploads/birmingham_petesfamous.pdf.

Hilliard, Emily. "Slaw Abiding Citizens: A Quest for the West Virginia Hot Dog." *Gravy* 61 (Fall 2016).

Korfhage, Matthew, and Denise Watson. "'The last real yock': Chinese soul-food restaurants are closing in Hampton Roads." *The Virginian-Pilot*, August 17, 2018, https://pilotonline.com/life/flavor/restaurants/article_171102a2 -a008-11e8-ac0b-a7a26bbe137d.html.

Reed, John Shelton, and Dale Volberg Reed. *Holy Smoke: The Big Book of North Carolina Barbecue*. Chapel Hill: University of North Carolina Press, 2008.

Wood, Sara. "Patsy Wong Oral History," Portsmouth, Virginia, May 23, 2014. Southern Foodways Alliance, https://www.southernfoodways.org/app /uploads/Wong-Patsy_SFA-WOOD_21May2014.pdf.

## GAS

Fratesi, Mark. Phone conversation with the author, October 7, 2017.

Jakle, John A., and Keith A. Sculle. *The Gas Station in America*. Baltimore, MD: Johns Hopkins University Press, 1994.

Medley, Kate. "Meat and Three & Ten Dollars' Worth of Regular." *Bitter Southerner*, November 11, 2014, http://bittersoutherner.com/meat-and -three-and-ten-dollars-worth-of-regular/#.Ww3A8Kkh1mA.

Medley, Kate, and Emily Wallace. "At the gas station, biscuits, tortillas—and community." *Indy Week*, February 8, 2012, https://www.indyweek .com/indyweek/at-the-gas-station-biscuits-tortillasand-community /Content?oid=2796071.

Ozersky, Josh. *Colonel Sanders and the American Dream*. Austin: University of Texas Press, 2012.

Smith, Andrew F., ed. *The Oxford Companion to American Food and Drink*, s.v. "Convenience Store." New York: Oxford University Press, 2007.

Wolfe, Anna. "Hunger: Food desert in Mississippi Delta impacts health." *Clarion Ledger*, September 24, 2017, https://www.clarionledger.com/story/news/politics/2017/09/24/hunger-food-desert-mississippi-delta-impacts-health/588052001/.

## HYPERBOLE

Paul, Dave. Phone interview with the author, May 1, 2018.

Handwerker, William. *Nathan's Famous: The First 100 Years, an Unauthorized View of America's Favorite Frankfurter Company*. New York: Morgan James Publishing, 2016.

Hurley, Terry. Phone interview with the author, May 1, 2018.

Rodgers, Wanda. Phone interview with the author, May 2, 2018.

Sanderson, Bud. Phone interview with the author, April 27, 2018.

Turner, Carolette Cromer, and Rob Cromer. Interview with the author, August 19, 2017, Columbia, South Carolina.

## ICONS

Edge, John T. *The Potlikker Papers: A Food History of the Modern South*. New York: Penguin Press, 2017.

Kirby, Rachel C. "Mr. Peanut: Virginia's Agricultural Aristocrat." In *Southern Things: A Place, a People, and Its Things*, issue 4, Fall 2015 (Foodways), southernthings.web.unc.edu/mr-peanut.

Ozersky, Josh. *Colonel Sanders and the American Dream*. Austin: University of Texas Press, 2012.

Smith, Andrew F. *Peanuts: The Illustrious History of the Goober Pea*. Champaign University of Illinois Press, 2007.

## JUNQUE

Herman, Bernard L. "On Southern Things." *Southern Cultures* 23, no. 3 (Fall 2017): 7–13.

Hollis, Tim. *Dixie Before Disney: 100 Years of Roadside Fun*. Jackson: University Press of Mississippi, 1999.

Kennedy, Justin. Interview with the author, October 10, 2017, New Orleans, Louisiana.

Ownby, Ted. "Introduction: Thoughtful Souvenirs." In *Dixie Emporium: Tourism, Foodways, and Consumer Culture in the American South*, edited by Anthony J. Stanonis, 19–23. Athens: University of Georgia Press, 2008.

Revels, Tracy J. *Sunshine Paradise: A History of Florida Tourism*. Gainsville: University Press of Florida, 2011.

Stanonis, Anthony J., ed. *Dixie Emporium: Tourism, Foodways, and Consumer Culture in the American South*. Athens: University of Georgia Press, 2008.

Wilson, Charles Reagan. "A Helping of Gravy: Southern Food and Pop Culture." *Gravy* 54 (2015): 4–11.

Wilson, Charles Reagan. "Southern Tacky Anonymous: A Member in Good Standing." *Southern Living* 28 (February 1993): 178.

## KUDZU

Alderman, Donna G'Segner, and Derek H. Alderman. "Kudzu: A Tale of Two Vines." *Southern Cultures*, vol. 7, no. 3 (Fall 2001): 49–64.

Coates, Michael. Phone conversation with the author, May 1, 2017.

Cope, Channing. *Front Porch Farmer*. Atlanta, GA: T. E. Smith, 1949.

Edwards, Edith, and Henry Edwards. Interview with the author, August 1, 2017, Rutherfordton, North Carolina.

Finch, Bill. "The True Story of Kudzu, the Vine that Never Truly Ate the South." *Smithsonian Magazine*, September 2015, https://www.smithsonianmag .com/science-nature/true-story-kudzu-vine-ate-south-180956325/.

Pridmore, Robin. Phone conversation with the author, May 11, 2017.

## LANDMARKS

Gershon, Pete. *Painting the Town Orange: The Stories Behind Houston's Visionary Art Environments*. Charleston, SC: The History Press, 2014.

Jimmy Carter National Historic Site, Plains, Georgia, https://www.nps.gov/jica /index.htm.

Martin, William. "What's Red, White, and Blue . . . and Orange All Over?" *Texas Monthly*, October 1977, https://www.texasmonthly.com/articles /whats-red-white-and-blue-and-orange-all-over/.

Zucchino, David. "No need for alarm: South Carolina town's Peachoid water tower is getting a face-lift, that's all." *Los Angeles Times*, June 4, 2015, http://www.latimes.com/nation/la-na-peachoid-20150604-story.html.

## MEAT-AND-THREES

Cooley, Angela Jill. *To Live and Dine in Dixie: The Evolution of Urban Food Culture in the Jim Crow South*. Athens: The University of Georgia Press, 2015.

Egerton, John. *Southern Food: At Home, on the Road, in History*. New York: Alfred A. Knopf, Inc., 1987.

Lasseter, Mary Beth. "Ballery Tyrone Bully Interview," Jackson, Mississippi, April 9, 2014. Southern Foodways Alliance, https://www.southernfoodways .org/app/uploads/Tyrone-Bully_Bullys-Restaurant.pdf.

Penman, Susie. "Cracker Barrel's Culture: Exporting the South on America's Interstate Exits." Master's thesis, University of Mississippi, 2012.

## NACKETS

Bowers, Paige. "Tom's Foods." In *The New Georgia Encyclopedia*, October 6, 2006, edited June 16, 2013, www.georgiaencyclopedia.org/articles /business-economy/toms-foods.

Cahn, William. *Out of the Cracker Barrel: The Nabisco Story, from Animal Crackers to Zuzus*. New York: Simon & Schuster, 1969.

Cormier, Damon. Phone conversation with the author, May 1, 2018.

Evans, Amy. "Robert Cormier Interview," Scott, Louisiana, October 13, 2006. SouthernFoodways Alliance, https://www.southernfoodways.org/app/up- loads/BoudinTrail_TheBestStop.pdf.

McDaniel, Rick. "Coke and Peanuts: A Food Historian Speculates on How It Got Started." Coca-Cola Company, June 17, 2013, http://www.coca-colacompany .com/stories/coke-and-peanuts-a-food-historian-speculates-on-how-it -got-started.

"The Sandwich Story," Snyder's-Lance, Inc., accessed August 30, 2017, www .lance.com/the-sandwich-story.

Smith, Andrew F. *Peanuts: The Illustrious History of the Goober Pea*. Champaign: University of Illinois Press, 2007.

Wallace, Emily. "Orange You Glad." In *The Carolina Table*, edited by Randall Kenan, 88–91. Hillsborough, NC: Eno Publishers, 2016.

## OPEN

Dyer, Frank Lewis, and Thomas Commerford Martin. *Edison: His Life and Inventions*, Vol. 1. New York: Harper & Brothers Publishers, 1910.

Hurley, Andrew. "From Hash House to Family Restaurant: The Transformation of the Diner and Post-World War II Consumer Culture." *The Journal of American History*, Vol. 83, No. 4 (March 1997): 1282–1308.

Rawson, Katie. "'America's Place for Inclusion': Stories of Food, Labor, and Equality at the Waffle House." In *The Larder: Food Studies Methods from the American South*, edited by John T. Edge, Elizabeth Engelhardt, and Ted Ownby, 216–239. Athens: University of Georgia Press, 2013.

Wallace, Emily. "A beloved diner, Honey's closes for good." *Indy Week*, August 21, 2013.

Warner, Pat. Interview with the author, August 14, 2017, Atlanta, Georgia.

## PACKAGING

Carlin, Joseph M. "Waxed Paper." In *The Oxford Companion to American Food and Drink*, edited by Andrew F. Smith. New York: Oxford University Press, 2007.

Jones, Scott. Phone conversation with the author, May 27, 2017.

Mohan, Anne Marie. "KFC's sustainable sides container is 'sogood' [*sic*]." Greener Package, August 30, 2010, https://www.greenerpackage.com/reusability/kfc%E2%80%99s_sustainable_sides_container_sogood.

Oswald, Alison. "Boxed Up." Lemelson Center for the Study of Invention and Innovation, Smithsonian National Museum of American History, March 3, 2016, http://invention.si.edu/boxed.

Perry, Marge. "Packaging." In *The Oxford Companion to American Food and Drink*, edited by Andrew F. Smith. New York: Oxford University Press, 2007.

Smith, Andrew F. "Packaging." In *Food and Drink in American History: A "Full Course" Encyclopedia, vol. 1: A–L*, edited by Andrew F. Smith. Santa Barbara, CA: ABC-CLIO, 2013.

Wallace, Emily. "It Was There for Work: Pimento Cheese in the Carolina Piedmont." Master's thesis, University of North Carolina at Chapel Hill, 2010.

Williams-Forson, Pysche A. *Building Houses Out of Chicken Legs: Black Women, Food, and Power*. Chapel Hill: University of North Carolina Press, 2006.

## QUE

Auchmutey, Jim. *The New Encyclopedia of Southern Culture*, Vol. 7: *Foodways*, edited by John T. Edge, s.v. "Barbecue." Chapel Hill: University of North Carolina Press, 2007.

Edge, John T. *Southern Belly: A Food Lover's Companion*. Chapel Hill, NC: Algonquin Books, 2007.

Elie, Lolis Eric. *Cornbread Nation 2: The United States of Barbecue*. Chapel Hill: University of North Carolina Press, 2004.

Jakle, John A., and Keith A. Sculle. *Fast Food: Roadside Restaurants in the Automobile Age*. Baltimore: Johns Hopkins University Press, 1999.

Luster, Rachel Reynolds. "Robert Craig Interview," De Valls Bluff, Arkansas, August 1, 2010. Southern Foodways Alliance, https://www.southernfoodways.org/app/uploads/ArkansasBBQ_Craigs.pdf.

Reed, John Shelton, and Dale Volberg Reed. *Holy Smoke: The Big Book of North Carolina Barbecue*. Chapel Hill: University of North Carolina Press, 2008.

## ROADS

Hanchett, Tom. "A Salad Bowl City: The Food Geography of Charlotte, North Carolina." In *The Larder: Food Studies Methods from the American South*, edited by John T. Edge, Elizabeth Engelhardt, and Ted Ownby, 166–183. Athens: University of Georgia Press, 2013.

Ingram, Tammy. *Dixie Highway: Road Building and the Making of the Modern South, 1900–1930*. Chapel Hill: University of North Carolina Press, 2014.

Jones, May F., ed. *Public Letters and Papers of Locke Craig, Governor of North Carolina, 1913–1917*. Raleigh, NC: Edwards & Broughton Printing Company, State Printers, 1916.

Medley, Kate. "Hieu Pham Interview," Atlanta, Georgia, May 31, 2010. Southern Foodways Alliance, https://www.southernfoodways.org/app/uploads/AtlantasBufordHighway_Crawfish-Shack-Seafood.pdf.

Pham, Hieu. Phone conversation with the author, May 2, 2018.

Preston, Howard Lawrence. *Dirt Roads to Dixie: Accessibility and Modernization in the South, 1885–1935*. Knoxville: University of Tennessee Press, 1991.

Turner, Walter R. *Paving Tobacco Road: A Century of Progress by the North Carolina Department of Transportation*. Raleigh: North Carolina Office of Archives and History, 2003.

Walcott, Susan M. "Overlapping Ethnicities and Negotiated Space: Atlanta's Buford Highway." *Journal of Cultural Geography* 20 (2002): 51–75.

## STANDS

Chávez, Eduardo. Phone conversation with the author, May 1, 2018.

Cooley, Angela Jill. *To Live and Dine in Dixie: The Evolution of Urban Food Culture in the Jim Crow South*. Athens: University of Georgia Press, 2015.

Drinnon, Elizabeth McCants. *Stuckey: The Biography of Williamson Sylvester Stuckey, 1909–1977*. Macon, GA: Mercer University Press, 1997.

Jakle, John A., and Keith A. Sculle. *Fast Food: Roadside Restaurants in the Automobile Age*. Baltimore, MD: Johns Hopkins University Press, 1999.

Rosengarten, Dale. "Babylon Is Falling: The State of the Art of Sweetgrass Basketry." *Southern Cultures*, Vol. 24, No. 2 (Summer 2018): 98–124.

## TUNES

Garvey, Meaghan. "The Evolution of Playing Music in Your Car." *Complex*, February 10, 2015, http://www.complex.com/music/2015/02/the-evolution-of-playing-music-in-your-car/.

Hilliard, Emily. "Thursday Night Special," WXYC, Chapel Hill, NC.

Jones, JesseLee. Interview by Matt Campbell, "For the People," WSM, available at http://robertswesternworld.com.

Norman, Gail (longtime bartender at Robert's). Phone conversation with the author, May 23, 2018.

Riley, Sharon. "Record players were the infotainment systems of the 1950s and '60s: Early adventures in mobile fidelity." *Consumer Reports*, April 12, 2014, https://www.consumerreports.org/cro/news/2014/04/record-players -were-the-infotainment-systems-of-the-1950s-and-60s/index.htm.

Williams, Stephen. "For Car Cassette Decks, Play Time Is Over." *New York Times*, February 4, 2011, https://www.nytimes.com/2011/02/06/automobiles/06 AUDIO.html.

## UBIQUITY

Bledsoe, Jerry. "The Story of Hardee's." *Our State*, May 27, 2011, https://www .ourstate.com/hardees.

Cooley, Angela Jill. *To Live and Dine in Dixie: The Evolution of Urban Food Culture in the Jim Crow South*. Athens: University of Georgia Press, 2015.

Edge, John T. *The Potlikker Papers*. New York: Penguin Press, 2017.

Hardee, Wilber. *The Life and Times of Wilber Hardee*. New York: Writers Press Club, 2000.

Jakle, John A., and Keith A. Sculle. *Fast Food: Roadside Restaurants in the Automobile Age*. Baltimore, MD: Johns Hopkins University Press, 1999.

Johnston, J. Phillips L. *Biscuitville: The Secret Recipe for Building a Sustainable Competitive Advantage*. Westport, CT: Easton Studio Press, 2009.

Proctor, Mary Duncan. Phone call with the author, May 21, 2018.

Randall, Alice. "Glori-fried and Glori-fied: Mahalia Jackson's Chicken." *Gravy* 58 (Winter 2015): 32–37.

"SCLC Goes Into Chicken Business." *Philadelphia Tribune*, September 7, 1968.

## VACANCY

Belasco, Warren. *Americans on the Road: From Autocamp to Motel, 1910–1945*. Baltimore, MD: Johns Hopkins University Press, 1979.

Hobbs, Allyson. "The Lorraine Motel and Martin Luther King." *New Yorker*, January 18, 2016.

Jakle, John A., Keith A. Sculle, and Jefferson S. Rogers. *The Motel in America*. Baltimore, MD: Johns Hopkins University Press, 1996.

Thomas, Mark. Interview with the author, May 6, 2018, Savannah, Georgia.

## WINDOWS

Crosby, Thom. Interview with the author, June 20, 2017, Kingsport, Tennessee.

"The Future of Drive Thru: Overcoming Choke Points." *QSR*, August 2017, https://www.qsrmagazine.com/outside-insights/future-drive-thru-overcoming-choke-points.

Jakle, John A., and Keith A. Sculle. *Fast Food: Roadside Restaurants in the Automobile Age*. Baltimore, MD: Johns Hopkins University Press, 1999.

Langdon, Philip. *Orange Roofs, Golden Arches: The Architecture of American Chain Restaurants*. New York: Alfred A. Knopf, 1986.

Sparkman, Donna. Phone conversation with the author, April 17, 2018.

Taylor, Bill. "How One Fast-Food Chain Keeps Its Turnover Rates Absurdly Low." *Harvard Business Review*, January 26, 2016, https://hbr.org/2016/01/how-one-fast-food-chain-keeps-its-turnover-rates-absurdly-low.

Vaughn, Daniel. "The History of the Pig Stands: 'America's Motor Lunch.'" *Texas Monthly*, February 18, 2015, https://www.texasmonthly.com/bbq/the-pig-stands/.

## XXX

Bruce, Kenny. "Junior Johnson: Last American Hero 50 Years Later." April 6, 2015, www.nascar.com/en_us/news-media/articles/2015/4/6/junior-johnson-nascar-history-kenny-bruce.html.

Dedman, Dixon. Phone conversation with the author, August 4, 2017.

Hoppe, Graham. "Does the Moon Shine on Legal Moonshine?" Blog post, May 31, 2016, https://www.southernfoodways.org/does-the-moon-shine-on-legal-moonshine.

Ingram, Tammy. *Dixie Highway: Road Building and the Making of the Modern South, 1900–1930*. Chapel Hill: University of North Carolina Press, 2016.

Pierce, Daniel S. *Real NASCAR: White Lighting, Red Clay, and Big Bill Frace*. Chapel Hill: University of North Carolina Press, 2010.

## YONDER

Compton, Betsy, and Tony Luker. Interview with the author, August 15, 2017, Jefferson, Alabama.

"Cooper's Country Store." ETV Shorts, *South Carolina Educational Television*, April 1, 2016, https://www.scetv.org/blog/etv-shorts/2016/coopers-country-store.

Harris, Jenni. Phone conversation with the author, April 13, 2018.

Kennedy, Hunter. "Cooper's Country Store." *Garden & Gun*, December/January 2014, https://gardenandgun.com/articles/our-kind-of-place-coopers-country-store.

McKenna, Maryn. "White Oak Pastures' General Store is the first retail store to openin Bluffton in more than 40 years." *Atlanta*, October 13, 2016, http://www.atlantamagazine.com/dining-news/white-oak-pastures-general-store-first-retail-store-open-bluffton-40-years/.

Thompson, Edgar T. "Country Store." In *Encyclopedia of Southern Culture*, edited by William R. Ferris and Charles Reagan Wilson. Chapel Hill: University of North Carolina Press, 2009.

## ZEALOTS

Franklin, Aaron. Interview with the author, October 13, 2017, Austin, Texas.

McGinn, Dave. "Drawing the line: What drives us to wait in huge lineups for a taste of the latest food trend?" *The Globe and Mail*, August 11, 2015, https://www.the globeandmail.com/life/food-and-wine/food-trends/the-lengths-well-go-to-what-drives-us-to-wait-in-line-for-the-latest-food-trend/article 25924683, updated June 5, 2017.

Stone, Alex. "Why Waiting Is Torture." *New York Times*, August 18, 2012, https://www.nytimes.com/2012/08/19/opinion/sunday/why-waiting-in-line-is-torture.html.

York, Joe. "André Prince Jeffries Interview," July 7, 2006, Nashville, Tennessee, https://www.southernfoodways.org/app/uploads/Nashville-Eats_Princes-Hot-Chicken_Andre-Jeffries.pdf.

# INDEX OF PLACES

*Note: This list does not include national chains, large theme parks with a national profile, or establishments that have closed.*

ABOUT THE AUTHOR

Born and raised in North Carolina, Emily Wallace is the art director and a deputy editor for the quarterly journal *Southern Cultures* and a freelance writer and illustrator. Her work has appeared in the *Washington Post*, *Oxford American*, *Southern Living*, and other publications.